Mystic Saints Of India:4

Saint Kabir

B. K. CHATURVEDI

Series Editor : Dr. Mahendra

BOOKS FOR ALL
Delhi-110052

Distributed by :
D. K. Publishers Distributors Pvt. Ltd.
1, Ansari Road,
New Delhi-110 002
Phs. : 327 8368, 326 1465
Fax : 326 4368
E-mail : dkpd@del3.vsnl.net.in
Web site:www.dkpd.com.

First Published : 2000

ISBN 81-7386-233-8 (Saint Kabir)
ISBN 81-7386-231-1 (Series)

Published by :
Books For All
B-2, Vardhaman Palace,
Nimri Commercial Centre,
Near Ashok Vihar Phase-IV,
Delhi-110 052
Ph. : 740 1672, 745 2453
E-mail : lpp@nde.vsnl.net.in
Web site:www.lppindia.com.

Printed at :
D. K. Fine Art Press Pvt. Ltd.
Delhi-110052 Ph. 745 2451

Printed in India

SERIES' EDITOR'S NOTE

In 1963, Dr. Radhakrishnan, the President of India, declared in Bombay, " The time has come for all countries to work towards making the world a single home for Humanity.....Economics, Politics and transport have done their jobs. But we have to do as to give a soul to the world which has found a body, you can give it if you are truly Indian." We Indians are proud to have so many mystic saints in our history who can contribute the upliftment of the human being.

In Indian thinking, there are two modes in which we acquire knowledge: Argument and Experiment. Both these modes, together with experience play an important role in the development of mankind. Saints of India, through their arguments, tried to communicate their experiences to human beings. This represent an adventure in thinking.

This series, it is hoped, will enable the reader, eastern or western, to understand and appreciate currents of Indian thoughts by depicting the life and writings of different saints, we have tried to portray the true picture of Indian Culture. I am really thankful to all those, who have helped in preparing and publishing these books, as it will not only propagate the ideas of Indian saints, but also help in making the mankind a better race.

Our world, becomes wider, our imagination richer and our life more colourful and more gestful as the result of our companionship with these saints, who are the travellers of the spirit and the pioneers of thought.

25.7.99 **(DR.) MAHENDRA**

Contents

Preface

Kabir was essentially a reformer and it was a sheer chance that he chose poetry as the medium of communicating his views and thoughts. Perhaps he was helpless because it was the crying need of the times that had chose him as the medium to express their agonies. Kabir attained that unique status in society because he had the courage to say all those grim facts which the era longed earnestly for. In a sense, perhaps, his supposed illiteracy or lack of education proved to be a strong weapon in his hand since his ideas had no transmission-loss due to sophistry of language. His observations appear to emerge from the core of the heart. At times his crudity of language hits you with an inescepable blow.

The attempt in this present work has been to cover Kabir as comprehensively as possible with in the given space. That is why the main emphasis has been on his poems since they reveal his thoughts much better than the various commentaries on him. Also, since there is no authentic versions of his biography only those events of his life has been culled which are referred to in his poetic creations. The country is gratefully celebrating his 600th anniversary and it was found to be apt to add this shall flower of tribute from our side.

The author is ineffably grateful to Mittal brothers of 'Books For All' for giving him an opportunity to write freely and frankly on Kabir.

-B.K. Chaturvedi

I. Kabir : A unique poet Thinker of Iconoclastic mould

An iconoclastic poet is apparently a contradiction in terms. But Kabir was such a poet who blasted all blasphemous superstitious with a relentless zeal and opposed every faith and belief, based on the diehard dogmas sans practical logic. Why poetry and iconoclasm appear self-contradictory because poetry invariably resorts to imagination while inconoclastic insistence is on striking the hard reality. If any one could coordinate the two with such finesse as to be remembered even 600 years after his death,surely he was an extraordinary person. What adds to his achievement is the fact that he was thoroughly illiterate. Yet he could place the words so beautifully as to convey his profound thoughts whose incisiveness remains unblunted even after six hundred years. His thoughts created a definite school of followers who are still in existence and known as 'Kabir Panthis'. It is a different matter that invariably such followers of an iconoclastic ideology create a blaspheme for themselves and hence lose their significance in the main stream of life. Nevertheless, their leaders like Kabir's contribution in building the general ethos of a major part of the country can not be gainsaid.

As a matter of fact, when Kabir became conscious of the times he was living in [at the middle of the 14th century - he is believed to have been born in 1400 A.D.] the political, social and economical condition of the country were appalling. Various Sultans had come to rule Delhi for short duration without any one of them getting easy stability of the kind that the Mughal rule had enjoyed. With the seat of political authority remaining shaky there was no control over administration. Jungle law was prevailing all around and the common masses were feeling insecure on all counts. History bears testimony to the fact that when the people, particularly of the orient - feel disenchanted with secular authority they invariably look heavenwards for relief. Hence the cult of Bhakti (devotion to God) which started gaining momentum at the time when Kabir came into this world.

Socially the situation was getting quite anarchic and confused. Although the Muslim population had begun to intermingle with local population, by this time it was that the social equations could begin to develope between them. But the inborn xenophobia had also began to show its effect in the alarming proportions. With the political authority beginning to pass into the hands of the outsiders who initially came as invaders and subsequently started to be associated with the land they once desired to capture, the social tensions became more and more pronounced. Each section started denouncing the other as inferior. This disintegrating process not only created schim in the main faith, like Hinduism and Islam but also crevices began to appear in the various sects and communities that developed within one fold of faith. Among the Hindus the subsections : Shaakta, Shaiva and Vaishnavas had started taking cudgels against each other and the Muslims also began to be pronouncedly divided among the Shias, Sunnis etc.....

In fact this was the time when the whole country had become quite distablished. The common population began to be severely inflicted with mutual rivalry among the various centres of the self proclaimed authority. Seeing the secular representatives of the divine authority behaving in the most callous and parochial way the people had no where to go but to indulge in deeper prayer to the Almighty to set again the chaos in order. This led to the growth of various poet-thinker-philosopher seeking recourse in pure devotion. Kabir was among the pioneers who almost recommenced the Bhakti movement by his iconoclastic poems.

Kabir is renowned for his tirade against pretensions. Anyone who had even a little difference between his convictions and practice was the target of Kabir; whether he be a Muslim or Hindu. This inborn prejudice against false pretensions was developed by kabir in strong reaction to whatever he saw in the society around him. Since his place of living was Benaras(Kashi or Varanasi) which was a sort of confluencing point of prophets from every state of India owing to it being the most hallowed city, he could meet many persons adhering to different faith and cultures. But as the general trend was during his period he detected a streak of falsehood among the various adherents of different faiths. This made him anti-regimentation and he started preaching the liberty of the soul. He began to impress upon the people that the religious regimentations or communities created diversions in the society owing to their personal and selfish intents. Else, he argued, going by the basic truth that each faith disseminated, it is one and the same. In fact Kabir himself was influenced by the Sufism which also preached that the ultimate reality enshrined in every faith pointed to the same basic fact : that God is one; He is benevolent and kind to all beings. When he wrote:

Kaaba phir Kashi bhaya,
Ramahu bhaya Raheem
Moth Choona maida bhaya,
Bhaitha Kabeera jeem!

his idea was no different to what Mirja Ghalib wrote many centuries later :

Hum muhavvida hain hamara kesh hai tarque-rusoom
Millaten jah mita gayeen, azza-e-iman ho gayeen!

(We believe in one God and our religion is shedding all communal belief; for when the communal preferences vanish we see the real element of faith)

Kabir was a votary of faith which had only two entities : the lover and the beloved. Like the Sufis he also believed the soul to be wife of the Supreme Being. He calls Raja Ram (God) as his 'bharataar' i.e. the husband who sustains his spouse. For him the soul's ultimate destination is coalescence with the Supreme Being. When he sees the world permeated by only the lover and the Beloved he laments over the superficial distinctions being made. He always preaches that the material possessions are of transitory significance. He was a fearless fellow ever immersed in the bliss of his beholding his Beloved. Carefree and straightforward he despised all that cloaked the real vision of the self to visualise Self. In his iconoclastic vein he derided all kind of categorisation. He was against the castiest categorisation as well. He claimed that no one was untouchable or lowly and of higher caste by birth. All these divisions, to him, were the outcome of the crass selfishness of man. He claims :

Hum tumha manhi ekei lohoo,
Ek paani jeevan hai mohvoo,
Ekehi janani janyan samsā rā ,
Kon gyā n se bhaye ninara?

(It is only one quality of blood that circulates in everybody and each body is instinct with same vital force. All are the product of same nature. Then how can man be distinguished from other.)

He was also very practical in his approach. He denounced all those rituals that enhance the discrimination between man and man. He was very much against the iconolatory. With concealed sarcasm he wrote :

Pāthar pooje hari mile
tan main poojoon pahar,
Tā sen to chakiyā bhalee
Jo pees-khai sansā r!!

(If worship of stones can lead one to Hari (God) why shouldn't we worship mountains (which have greater amount of stone). Or better, we should worship our stone-grinder, which grinds cereals for us and gives us food to eat.)

He believed that it is our bounded duty to stay in total harmony with each other. He despised in the strongest terms the communities that created various divisions in society. His claim is :

Sarvabhoota ekei kari janya, chooka vad-vivara |
Kahi Kabir man poora paya, bhaye Ram parisara ||

(When it is the One Entity that breeds all why must the debates and arguments should continue erroneously. Says Kabir that in himself he found Ram and only Ram permeating everywhere and so be true with others as well.)

He repeatedly expressed the same thought in his poems that God is one and He is omnipresent. Confining His abode in any one particular place is the attempt of the confused minds. He stresses that instead of making Ram and Raheem as one's own it is any time better to surrender yourself unto them. It is because it is always the drop that confluences with the ocean and never the vice-versa. Complete surrender unto Himself is the duty of every man and the message beamed by every faith. He says that it appears that the whole world has turned mad. While the Muslims claim that Raheem is theirs the Hindus proclaim that Ram is theirs, little realising that both Ram and Raheem are no different and identical.

"Hindu kahat hain Rām hamārā ,
Muselmān Rehmānā
Apas men donon larhe marat hain,
maram na koi pahichānā "

While kabir strongly attacked the Hindus for perpetrating religious superstitions and rituals he didn't spare the Muslims either. Deriding the Muslims practice of sacrificing goat and claiming this to be enjoined by their faith he asked :

"Jeeva badhat aur dharam kahat ho
adharam kahan hai bhai;
Āpan tan mani jan hai baithe,
Kāsan kahon kasai"

(You slaughter a being and call this to be a part of your religious duty, then, pray, tell me, what else is unrighteous conduct? If you insist on yourself being called a saintly figure because of this sacrifice, who should I call to be a butcher?)

Kabir's faith was a faith based on pure love. It is a call for universal brotherhood. He was also against those books which make man bigoted. He says :

"Pothi padhi-padhi jag muaa pundit bhayā na koi
Dhai akhar prem ka padhe jo pandit hoi"

He believed that it is the same light that radiates from every soul.

What adds to the surprise of a lay reader is the fact that traditionally he is said to be totally illiterate. Although his repeated emphasis on recognising the real knowledge hidden in the two letters 'Ra' and 'Ma' blatantly refutes this theory of his being illiterate, (His poems prove that he could read and write) yet he has himself claimed that 'Masi kagad chuyo nahin haath' (I have never touched paper and ink). That fact makes him still greater because whatever he has said is borne by his own experience. He too claims

"Tum tau kahat kagad ki lekhi
Kabir kahat akhin ki dekhi"

(You stand by what you have seen written on paper while I adhere to what I have seen with my own eyes.)

Kabir's views on religious bigotry, superstition and discriminatory belief transcend the limits of time and space. In fact his teachings have their distinct school with a set of followers still active around Kashi. It is believed that it was his teachings that influenced as different persons as Nanak in 15th century in undivided Punjab and Rabindranath Tagore in 20th century in Bengal. In fact the holy book of the Sikhs : 'Guru-Grantha-Sahib' has a lot of his poems. Imagine the impact of his views that many of his thoughts have become a part of the religious text of a dynamic faith! It is because what he stresses on is the obvious though clouded by the egoistic considerations of certain doctrines.He was a very revolutionary poet of his own time.

Surprisingly, apart from what is revealed about his life by his various Dohas(also called Saakhee because they reflect his observation with the Saakshee or witness being God Himself) and 'padas', there is no authentic biography available of him. Perhaps he remained so deeply engrossed in ameliorating the agony of his suffering society that he never cared writing much about his own self. Nevertheless, what is available in his works and legends about his life is given in the pages ahead. Although there is still much confusion about his personal details what has been built as his life-story is based upon the most authenticated events of his life as revealed by his works.

II. Birth Legends

Historians, literateurs and the followers of the cult started by Kabir himself widely differ on his date of birth.Even the fact has not yet been finally decided as to he was a Hindu or Muslim. Various legends have been interwoven to clear these doubts and establish authenticity. Some of them are given below.

Legends Related to His Birth

(i) About 600 years ago there lived a poor weaver in Kashi(modern Varanasi or Banaras). His name was Neeru.Owing to his poor conditions he was unmarried because in his caste bride's father expected somthing solid from the groom in exchange of giving his daughter in marriage. Gradually with much difficulty and hard labour he could save as much as money as to enable him to marry. He was eventually married to a village close to the historic city of Kashi. Although most of the marraige conditions has been fulfiled some still remained.Only after fulfiling them that he could take his wife to his home.Neeru was desperate. He was particularly expert in weaving cloth of coarser variety which was the favorite of the Sadhu's and the nobleman. That cloth, though by appearance and touch appeared very rough, was long lasting.

That was the reason why the noble man prefered that cloth. Once dyed in the ochre colour it would continue to cover their bodies for long durations while surviving the violent beating when they washed it.

Fortunately for Neeru, Kashi suddenly had a population explosion. Not much time had elapsed to the northen part of the country getting plundered and devasted by Timur, the lame. The fear and panic continued to haunt the population. Since in distress God is remembered most, people started thronging at the holy places to seek God's protection. Kashi, being the highest holy tirtha of the region, had become crowded by people coming from even far off places. Owing to the tremendous enhancement in population, Neeru could do a roaring business. He soon managed to get the remaining money to conclude his marriage, by performing the ceremony of 'Gona' to bring his wife home.

Eventually he left the village with his wife after 'Gona' to repair to Kashi. Since he was too poor to afford the fare of a bullock drawn vehicle, he decided to cover the distance on foot with his wife, Neema. She was also a sturdy girl and didn't mind walking though she was afraid that her new dress might be spoilt by the travails of the on-foot journey.

Though they left the village early, they began to feel the scorching heat of the sun even when they had covered only half of their way. In order to take rest and refresh themselves they stayed beneath a tree close to the famus 'Laharatara pond'. While washing their face and hands suddenly Neema heard the sound of a weeping child. She told Neeru : 'Don't you hear a child crying - almost an infant, as revealed by its voice!'

Neeru had also heard the sound. Out of curiousity

he followed the sound to its source. Their he found an infant lying amidst the bushes and crying its heart out. It appeared to have been born not long time back. Neema was also watching the crying infant - a very cute and lovable being. The infant's eyes beshone as though gems had been set in the eyes' socket.

Neema was unsure as to what to do? Taking the infant along might create some problem, she thought. After all, how would she convince the people about her chastity before her marriage? Neeru was thinking on the same lines. At last they made a resolve to take the child along, caring two hoots for the people's opinion.

It is believed that Neeru's old house was situated in the locality in Kashi still known as 'Kabir - Chaura'. When they reached home people were surprised to see the young couple arriving home with a child also between them. No doubt some questions were asked but Neeru - Neema concocted a false story. The people also were so enchanted seeing the unusually thoughtful visage of the infant that they eventually dropped the probing about the infant's real origin.

After some days when the things had quietened a bit, Neeru requested a Quazi to grace his hut and baptise the boy with a good name. As per the age-old practice among the adherents of Islam, the Quazi reached them and opened the Holy Book at random to select a name for the boy. As the coincidence or perhaps the divine scheme would have it, every time the Quazi opened a page his finger touched only the renowned synonyns of God, like Kubra, Kabir, Akbar etc.

The Quazi was amazed. Yet his every attempt made his fingre touch a similar synonym of God.

" Is it an indication from Holy Allah?" he asked himself. Hearing this news many other learned Quazis also gathered but their learned attempts couldn't offer any name of different category for the infant. One or two also grew apprehensive lest this should be an indication of the approaching doom. "You better get rid of this boy. He appear accursed!" But undaunted by their chilling advise, both Neeru and Neema held firm and refused to part with the boy. They began to nurture that boy lovingly. He began to be called Kabir. Nobody could have expected that one day this boy of unknown parentage would be reckoned as India's most widely discussed and admired poet-thinker.

(ii) Their is yet another leagend popular among the Hindus which seeks to fill the gaps in among the above mentioned leagend. It is said that one day a brahmin of Kashi went to seek blessings of the renowned sage Swami Ramananda. He also had his widowed young daughter following him. Along with the father that widowed daughter touched Swami Ramananda's feet. Ramananda was lost in his divine communion. Unmindfully he also blessed the daughter by saying : "May you beget a noble son!" Since the legend sage's word couldn't be untrue, it is said that after some time the widowed daughter begot the son. That was nothing short of commiting a social sacrilege! How could a widowed woman beget a son? Accusing finger began to be raised at her. She felt so disturbed that hardening her heart she decided to get rid of her unwanted son.

Eventually one night she left her home quietly and abondonded the child near the famous pond Lahar-tara. Subsequently Neema and Neeru saw that infant and brought the infant home.

These legends do indicate as though Kabir was brought into the world by a Hindu widow but he was brought up by a Muslim weaver couple. Perhaps that was the reson why Kabir developed so much of rancour towards the false notions afflicting both the faiths. All Kabir's writings indicate his being very much adhering to two faiths sans their dogmatic and pretentive practises. In him two faiths appear so deeply intermingled that it is difficult to identify which of them he really adhered to.

(iii) The third legend regarding his birth appears to be a part of a mythological story. It claims that Kabir was the reincarnation of saint Shukadeva. We all know that Shukadeva was the son of sage Ved-vyas of the Mahabharata fame and he was born wise. Even before his completing his twelve years he had mastered all the scripture and Vedas. His mastering over 'Srimad Bhagwat' is believed to be legendary. When Parikshit, the son of Abhimanyu, was hidding in his palace to escape the curse of high sage and thinking that has end of nigh, he requested sage Ved-Vyas to do something as to ensure his place in the heavens. Then Ved-Vyas had asked his son, Shukadeva, to recite to Parikshit the Shrimad Bhagwat to ensure the accursed decendant of the Pandavas gettig a niche in the heavens.

Whatever be the truth, it is claimed that Shukadeva reincarnated himself as Kabir on the instructions of Lord

Mahadeva. It may be reminded that in his earlier birth Shukadeva had remained in the womb of his mother for about twelve years. In order to escape the travails of coming into the world through a human womb, this time his embryo was put in an oyster-shell and that shell was floated in the Ganga. From the Ganga that shell reached the Lahar-tara pond where it appeared as a very lovely infant.

Infact, all these legends reveal as if nothing is finally known about Kabir's birth. They also point out that this boy was born in the most unusual circumstances. As a matter of fact, all of them appear as interpolations concocted later on to justify the extra-ordinary existence of Kabir. Even his birth-day is still clouded in confusion. However, a legendary 'Doha' indicate that he was born around 1399-1400 A.D. as it says :

"Chaudaha sau pachapan sal gaye,
Chandrawar ek thath thaye |
Jeth sudee Barasayat kon
Pooranmasi prakat bhaye ||"

That is after the expiry of the Vikram Samvat 1455, he was born on Monday on the full moon day of Jeystha month, on the festival day of Vat-Savitri. Although Kabir-Panthis still celebrate his day of birth on Vat -Savitri day, the scholars on the basis of certain astrological calculations found out that the actual day of Kabirs birth should be the Vat-Savitri day of the year 1456 Vikram Samvat since the Doha claims that he was born after the expiry of the Vikram year 1455 which means in 1456. The government's record also give his year of birth to be 1456 Vikram Samvat i.e.,

1400 A.D.

In fact the place of his birth has not yet been finally ascertained. There are three theories which argue that his place of birth could either be Maghahar, Kashi or a small village Belahara in district Azamgarh in U.P.

The plea favouring his birth Maghahar takes recourse to one line by Kabir, asserting:

Pahilen darsan Maghahar payo
Puni Kashi base aayee!

(First he saw Maghahar in the world and then migrated to Kashi). Maghahar is the place near Kashi where his mousoleum still stands. It is believed that he quitted his mortal coil at this place.

Although Kashi appears to be the place he had lived most, there is no specific evidance to support his birth at Kashi apart from the name of a locality. And about the Belahara village in Azamgargh the fact is that even this place has not yet been deciphered. Some claim that it was Belahara which later acquired the name Lahar-tara but there is no supporting evidence either. In fact in Azamgarh district there is neither any building traditionally associated with Kabir's name nor there is any Akhara of the Kabir-panthis.

Going by all the available material and legends, it appears logical to accept that Kabir had been born, bred and brought up only at Kashi.

III. Important Events of Life

His becoming Swami Ramananda's Disciple

Kabir began to grow up in Kashi. He was totally different from the boys of his age. He had neither much interest in games nor in studies. His parent didn't either had much money to send him to any school or Madarsa. As mentioned before, his parents were quite poor and it was difficult to make both ends meet for them. With the result Kabir formally didn't receive any regular education. But does one need any outer enlightenment whose soul be already radiating the divine light. Although he has himself confessed:

"Masi kagad chhoyo nahin,
kalam gahee nahin haath!"

It is difficult to believe that he was totally illiterate. If he was so how could he know that for writing the word 'Ram' you need to use two letters 'Rā' and 'm'. Moreover, how could he know that for writing the word 'Prem' two and half letters (in Nagari) are needed. It appears logical to believe that though he had not received any formal education, he was not illiterate. In fact, Kashi's atmoshphere, even other wise is so instinct with knowledge that even without formal education he was quite knowledgeable. As a matter of fact, many similes and metaphors that he employed in his poems appear to have been translated from Sanskrit scriptured text. The doha 'Saat samand ki masi karon'(full text is given in the translation section) is just a literal translation of the Vedic prayer. So it can be safely assumed that he had some basic education by his own efforts though he never attended any school.

Right from the childhood, boy Kabir had different attitude. Instead of playing games or enjoying his time in the similar pursuits, or enjoying his time in the similar pursuits, he used to sit on the bank of the river Ganga, quietly gazing at the flow of the current and observing the world quite dispassionately. His writings reveal his keen insight. However, from day one he was devoted to God. Call it Ram or Allah he was in total communion with that Spirit. Surprisingly, dispite living in a poor Muslim weaver's house, he was found bearing the Tilak on his forehead like the Hindus did. And he always chanted the name of Ram, to the great chagrin and annoyance of the fellow Muslims.

As Kabir started growing up he realised the need of having a Guru. He appeared to have learnt at a very tender age that a rudderless boat reaches no destination.

In Kashi, Acharya Swami Ramananda was the most famous holy man in those days. But he was a devout Vaishnava and how could he have initiated the son of a lowly Muslim weaver? Although Kabir tried his best to reach near Ramananda he was repeatedly prevented. However, during his efforts to reach near his desired Guru, he had learnt about his routine. Kabir had learnt that every day before the day-break Ramanada Swami came to the ghat of Ganga to have his bath. Having learnt the route his Guru was expected to come by, Kabir went ahead and before the day break lay himself flat on one of the steps leading to the Ganga. When Ramananda was climbing the steps after his Ganga-bath, his foot happened to be placed on the body of some figure sprawling on that step. Ramananda was imbalanced a bit but saying 'Ram-Ram' he removed his foot from that figure who was no one else but Kabir himself. Kabir accepted that 'Ram-Ram' as the holy mantra given by his Guru. Right since that day he started claiming himself to he Ramananda Swami's disciple, Kabir himself propagated this fact.

When the high-caste Hindus learnt about Ramananda Swami accepting a lowly Muslim weaver as his disciple, they were furious. They led a delegation of the highly honoured Hindus to the Swami : "O Swami, "they asked: " How come you have accepted a lowly Muslim weaver as your disciple?" Ramananda Swami was surprised : "No I have not accepted any one as my disciple for many days now, lowly or high-cast one". But the leader of the deligation insisted. "Sir, that weaver-boy Kabir, keeps on claiming that you are his guru."

Swami ji assured the delegation that he would make a complete enquiry into the case next day morning he sent for the weaver boy:

"When did I accept you as my disciple, boy"? Why are you spreading this falsehood?"

Kabir replied in utter humility : " O Gurudev, you have accepted me as your disciple in totally a different way. While normally you impart the holy mantra of initition through the aspirants ears, in my case you did so by placing your foot on my body." Then Kabir narrated the whole incident. Hearing the details Swami Ramananda was touched to the core, 'How sincere and devoted is my this disciple'. Tears welled up in his eyes and he embraced Kabir ecstatically. Thenceforth Kabir began to be officially known as Ramananda's disciple.

His Facing Serve Opposition From Diehard Hindus and Muslims

As mentioned in the first chapter, the period in which Kabir was growing up was a era of great turmoil in India. Politically the "throne of Delhi had passed in to the hands of Muslim rulers though socially Muslim and Hindus were still a divided lot. Cultural dissimilarities and xenophobic considerations remained as real impediments in their unity. Since the Muslims had acquired political power they were torturing the Hindus. Both the major communities of north India had only hatred and hostility for each other. In these explosive conditions the Muslims felt poiquantly humiliated seeing one of their brethrens, a weaver's son living like a Hindu. Instead of remembering the holy name of Allah he was chanting only Ram's name. Not only that, he had started living like a Hindu as well. Kabir's 'infidelity' appeared for them as the major cause of rancour. The Muslims would often condemn Kabir by calling him 'Kaafir'. But undaunted, Kabir would counter their condemnation by saying : "Infidel are those that loof others' property; that dupe the guillible with dissimulation, that kill the beings in the name of religion".

In answering one of such charges he exhorts Quazi that " Cease misinterpretation of the Quoranic dictates and worship real God, O mad, or else you will be committing a great sacrilege. That is why I have sought the shelter of Ram whom I shall not leave no matter what you do to force me desert my real God."

Chhandi kateb Rām bhaja baure,
Julum karat hai bhāree !
Kabira pakarhi tek Rām ki,
Turuka rahe Pachhihāree !!

Although Kabir was taking on the imposters in has own way. his parent were also worried and they often admonished him " We are Muslims and follower of Allah. Why must you chant Ram's name? Why must you adopt to the Hindu rituals. Your disobeying our religious dictates will surely consign you to hell!"

But Kabir would argue: "What is the difference between Ram and Raheem? What is the difference between a Hindu and a Muslim. Both have similar body, similar system and almost similar blood circulating in their veins. And don't you see that even the religious teachings of both, the faiths proclaim almost the same truth. If sincerity to one's conviction leads one to hell, then that is the destination of my soul!"

So, no matter receiving advises from all quarters Kabir kept on moving on the path he deemed best. Meanwhile, his love for Ram continued to grow intenser and intenser. At times he would be so intoxicated in the wine of his Ram's name that he would forgo his worldly duties also. He would forget that he had to weave a full sheet.

Neema was quite worried seeing her son's this absent-mindidness. Often she would admonish Kabir : " How would you survive if you forget your works? How would you support your family? "Kabir had also become married by this time. But Kabir would explain : "Mother! When I put the thread in the needle-hole, all of a sudden I remember my Ram and forget everything else. But don't you worry. The one who has created this universe is also responsible for feeding it". He says this in one of his 'Padas'.

Kahat Kabir sunahu meri maayee!
Pooranhara tribhuvan rayee!!

However, thinking that when he would get married Kabir would develop greater sense of responsibility. With this idea in her mind Neema had arranged for his son's marriage. Later on, Kabir also got a son, called Kamaal.

Nevertheless he was still not bound by the family bonds. He had no consideration for worldly wealth because he knew that no matter what wealth one amassed, one couldn't take it with him to the next world. His idea was earning a wealth, which might also prove useful in the next life-like merit earned from the noble deeds. Even then he was conscious of his duty as a householder. He would everyday spin cloth, go to the market to sell it and supported his family with whatever income he received from his meager business. In the evening he would sit on the ghats of Ganga and listen to holy discourses. At times he would also attend to the 'Waaz' (the Muslim holy discourses). He never made any distinction between man and man. Whether the preacher was a high brahman or lowly pariah, if he found him to be revealing some fundamental truth of life, he would remain with that fellow for hours together.

One day a poor brahman reached near him when he was about to go to the market to sell his products. It was a freezing day and the poor brahman was scantily clad. He asked Kabir : "I need some cloth to cover my body. It is very cold and I have nothing to even cover my body properly. But I don't have much money". Feeling pity at the brahman's miserable condition Kabir decided to give half of the cloth sheet he had woven that day. He said : "O Brahman, all I can give you is half of this sheet. The remaining half sheet I would sell in the market to arrange food for my family."

The Brahman wasn't satisfied as only half sheet was hardly enough to cover his body. Eventually, out of sheer compassion Kabir gave that Brahman the full sheet. The poor man went away blessing Kabir profusely. As the Brahman left, the reality of this situation dawned on Kabir. "How would I feed my family to-day?" Brooding over the problem Kabir left for the Ganga Ghat. Although the day was over Kabir couldn't summon any courage to face his family. He kept sitting there, privately praying his Ram to offer some solution.

It was quite late in night that searching for his father, Kamal, happened to reach the Ganga Ghat.

"Abba! Why didn't you return home at your usual time? We are all worried. Then Amma sent me to search for you. Come home, we all are hungry". Kamal told him.

Kabir was stung to the quick when he heard "all are

hungry". He replied defensively : "Beta! I couldn't earn anything to buy food for you all. That was why I was avoiding going home. How to get food for you all?

Do, not worry for food", said Kamal reassuringly we have enough stock to provide us food two weeks?",

"Enough food ?" Kabir was amazed." "Where from it was arranged?" Kabir asked his son disbelievingly.

"Today a man came with a cart full of food items. He said that a king has sent it to Kabirdas's place with whom he was mightily pleased after hearing his discourse in the lane close to Vishwanath Temple".

"But to-day I couldn't go there since I had nothing to sell. It is in that lane that I sell most of my products". Kabir asked, rather incomprehensibly "I don't know", said Kamaal "But that fellow unloaded the entire stock at our home. He said that the Raja had sought your prior permission for sending the food-itmes"

Hearing about that mysterious Raja, Kabir couldn't check his tears. "That one would be no one else but Raja Ram, the sustainer of the entire world".

Then Kabir left for his home escorted by his son, Kamaal, singing his new composition : "Ek Kabira na muaa, jin ke Ram adhar!".

His faith in Ram's devotion grew much more firm. Although he was little unhappy that he seemed to have put this burden on his Ram- the burden of looking after his worldly needs as well.

Nevertheless, this incident added much to Kabir's widely spreading fame. People had now started listening to his views respectfully; many of them would even come to seek his blessings. Since Kashi, as always, had been a big religious centre frequented by other saints and holy men, Kabir's fame had started spreading outside Kashi as well. In fact it was his blunt and practical observartions that had started attracting the general masses' attraction. In an age steeped in confusion and doubt at least there emerged a light at the end of the dark tunnel.

However, his growing fame also bred many jealous persons. How could a society determining one's status by one's caste and riches could tolerate a lowly poor Muslim weaver getting so much of recognition in the holiest of holy city of Kashi? Not only the pundits but even the Maulavis and Mullah had become his sworn enemies.

First of all the high cast Brahmans held their conference to take the unanimous decision that this lowly weaver spreading blaspheme and untruth must be thrown out of the holy city of Kashi. The decision was widely circulated with city. The common masses who were discerning a kind of light emerging in their darkened minds were unhappy but they were too powerless in their disunited strength. Yet out of curiosity many gathered around Kabir's hut when the delegation of Brahman reached there to convey their decision.

Although Kabir was quite aware about their hostile intentions yet like a lowly weaver he treated them very respectfully and asked the reason of the augst members of

Kashi's learned society reaching his hut.

"A unanimous decision has been taken in our conference. According to it you must quit Kashi immediately", the leader of the Brahman delegation informed Kabir.

"But what crime have I committed to warrant such a severe punishment? What have I done to invite your wrath".

"This is our unanimous decision", declared the leader quite pompously. You must leave this holy city immediately".

"To the best of my knowledge", began Kabir humbly, "neither have I insulted any one nor committed any theft any where. I only chant Ram's name. I don't think it is a crime. At least I must be told what offense have I committed". Now the Brahman-leader said in a hurt voice : "Recently you treated even the lowly people(shoodras) lavishly on a sumptuous feast. But heaping humiliation on us, you never cared to invite any of us. Now the punishment of this negligence is....". All of a sudden some Brahmans reached near their leader and whispered something into his ear. The leader then resumed his declaration..... "either you treat us all even better than how you had treated the Shoodras or quit this city. Such defilers of our faith and system can not be permitted to stay any longer in Kashi".

Now this was blatant iniquity being perpetrated against innocent Kabir. Some people did raise a voice of protest but that proved to be a call in wilderness in the majority of greedy and gluttony Brahmans of Kashi. Kabir himself was perturbed since he was left with no food items to arrange another feast. The previous stock given by the mysterious king had exhausted. As was his nature, he never hoarded these things. When he found that he had more food-items' stock than was necessary he had fed the weak and the down-trodden lot of the city. Now the Brahmans wanted to be treated with great feast! Finding the solution to the problem beyond his foreseeable capability, he retired to his spot on the bank of the river Ganga. May be, some might call it a streak of escapism but for Kabir this meant non-identification with the self and reposing full confidence in the Self. He, though, did carry a guilt complex because deeply influenced by the psyche of his times, he felt that sending back the hungry Brahmans was not justifiable. But he had no means to fulfil their demand. So he retired quietly to his favorite spot along the Ganga-bank.

Meanwhile the delegation of the Brahmans was delighted inwardly that today it had exposed Kabir before the whole city. "Now he would know", some of them openly claimed "the consequence of dishonouring the Brahman of Kashi. The wrath of Lord Shankar would be soon befalling on him". Some predicted that he would soon face the attack of some deadly disease while other said that now the people of the city would themselves drive him out. "After all he has challenged the very order of our Sanatan Dharma".

While they were discussing this way, someone heheld a group of persons coming, carrying some load over their heads. There was also their leader who was guiding them, lo and behold, they found a huge stock of uncooked food items being unloaded before them. Maunds of maida(refined flour), rice, sugar, dry fruits etc. The leader of the group carrying the load, divided the whole lot into small heaps, each weighing about two and half seers of the choicest food items, topped by a dakshina[fees for the priest] of an anna. The mysterious leader immediately requested all the present Brahmanas to accept one lot as the gift from Kabirdas.

There was a wide spread commotion among the augst assembly of the 'noble' Brahmans? "How could that pauper arrange so many things so suddenly? And where is he?" But the wiser ones' among them advised them to accept their share and depart for there was no sense in asking any questions when they were getting their 'due share'.

But one of the curious Brahmans couldn't accept the gift quietly and he went in search of Kabir. Finding the saint on the bank of river he said in the vein of a light banter. "So you are sitting here quietly while the whole of Kashi is resounding with your glory? How could you arrange all the things so suddenly and so surreptitiously?"

Totally unaware of what had happened, Kabir asked : "What are you refering about ,O Brahman devta! What have I arranged so suddenly and so surreptitiously?"

Then the Brahman told Kabir all that had transpired following his exit from the scene. Kabir kept on listening quietly with tears of gratitude welling up in his eyes. Quietly he was saying to himself : "Ram is really kind. He always answers prayers made from a guileless heart. "Cheentee kee bhee neivar baje who bhee saheb sunata hai".

This incident took the wind out of the high-caste Hindus agitation against the teachings of Kabir. Many of them started becoming his followers.

But Kabir was not bothered about their obeying or disobeying whatever he said. He kept on observing his impressions in various poems that he composed. Now his poems also began to be sung by the common masses.

However, there was still one section of the society-the religious heads of the Muslim community : the Mullahs and the Maulavis – who were still against Kabir. What was adding to their discomfiture was Kabir's growing popularity among the Hindus despite being a lowly Muslim. They were seething with anger against this infidel of their faith. Although they tried their best to incite the local Hindus they couldn't succeed. Then they thought of marking their time. They had heard about the Delhi Sultan, Sikander Lodi visiting Kashi soon. They thought that now it would be better if they could incite the Muslim authority against this defiler of their faith.

IV. Confrontation With Sikandar Lodi

We all know that Sikandar Lodi reigned between 1488 to 1517 AD. He was the reigning Sultan of Delhi when Kabir's fame was spreading throughout the country. No doubt this sultan of Delhi was a tyrant but he was believed to the god-fearing and a faithful Muslim. Since Kashi or Benaras was also under his control, he decided to visit this part of his sultanate and set things right.

By this time Kabir, no doubt getting renown all over the country by his pithy observation and iconoclastic sarcasm against the deihard superstitions that had crept into both Hinus and Muslim faith, was an old man. Yet his ripening age had put in more firmness in his belief that these Mullahs, Maulvis and Pundits were defiling Hindu and Mulsim faiths by their arbitrary interpretations of the holy dictates injoined by each faith.

Although most of the Hindus had accepted Kabir as a saint cleansing the filth that had accummulated in to their faith, some of them were still against him. Couning with the Mullahs and Quazis they also reached before the Sultan with their complaints against the lowly weaver.

"Your Majesty", the chief Quazi submitted before the Sultan, "this lowly weaver doesn't accept any authority. He derides every religious head and abuses them openly. Despite being a Muslim he cares two hoots for all the dictates enjoined by the Holy Quran and tries to pose as though he himself is the messenger of Allah".

The Hindu Pundits also made their submission : "He is as dis-respectful to all our scriptures, the Vedas and Puranas and calls them a bundle of lies. Despite being a Muslim he marks his forehead with a holy 'Tilak' and chants the name of Ram, defiling our faith as well. We request your Majesty, that this fellow should be eliminated for the welfare of both society and faith". Sikandar Lodi was surprised to hear these complaints. Thus far he had either met the Hindus criticising Muslims or the Muslims critical of the Hindus. This was for the first time he found that both the communities critical of one old man believed to be a lowly weaver. He was himself curious to meet that person. So he asked his two sepoys to go to the address of this person and summon him to the royal presence.

Presently Kabir was summoned before him. A dark complexioned emaciated body which was scantily clad but which had eyes like two sparkling gems. Kabir's face registered no fear or fright of any kind. He even didn't ask the reason as to why he had been summoned to report before the Sultan. His face appeared totally indifferent to the surroundings. He didn't even greet the Sultan. Whereupon, the head Quazi said in an admonishing tone "Bow before the Sultan". Kabir replied : "I never bow before any Sultan or king enjoying authority for a few days. I bow only before the Sultan of all Sultans, my lord Ram". Kabir's apparently contumelious attitude filled Sultan's mind with anger. Blowing up in rage, the Sultan thundered.

"Hey you fool of a man? You are an infidel not before the divine authority but before the secular authority as well.

You puke abuses against all religious dictates as enjoined by our Holy Books. You defy both the faiths. Which faith do you really belong to?".

"I am a man not bound by religious limits. My faith is welfare of humankind", Kabir replied, quite undaunted by the royal authority.

"It appears you have nothing to say in your defence", the Sultan said in a threatening voice.

"Why should I offer any argument in my defence when I have committed no crime", Kabir replied non-challantly.

"Blaspheme is the greatest crime under my rule. You are spreading it. Do you deny it?"

"I have said all I had to. I am spreading no blaspheme but only truth;" Kabir was as defiant as ever before any authority.

"So, you accept the charge", the Sultan asked finally.

"If speaking truth, calling a vice a vice is a crime, I shall ever be committing it. Lot of vices have infiltrated in to every faith and cleansing them is my right. When I tell people that they are being misled by Mullahs and Pundits for the sake of their serving their selfish end, it is a fact and no crime", Kabir replied fearlessly. The Sultan was rather impressed by Kabir's fearlessness. He further said : "Can you be little more specific in laying your counter charges against the Mullahs and Pundit?"

Kabir then lapsed into poetry to lay the charge :

"Yeh sab jhoonthee bandagi
Birtha pancha niwaj,
Sanche maare jhothi padhi
Quazi kair akaj"

[All this is sham-worship and useless way of saying the prayers. The Quazi tries to kill truth by following falsehood]

Kabir launched his broadside against the Mullah as well.

Quazi Mullah bharamiya, chalya duni ke sath
Dil the deem bisariya, karad layee jah haath"

[When the Quazi and Maulavi took the knife in their hands to butcher beings, they deviated from the rightious path. Now they follow the world and not the essence of their faith]

Kabir's straight-forwardness was transparent. He had nothing to hide from anyone, be that man or a Sultan. He further said : "I have nothing against any one. I worship only my Lord Ram as ordained by my Guru. For me there is no difference between man and man".

In consultation with the Quazi, the royal order was conveyed : "Since he has denounced Islam, rub off the mark from his forehead and stone him to death! He is an infidel, who refuses to believe in Islam".

Kabir retorted : "Me a Kafir! It is you all. Which

faith enjoins you to slaughter a cow, cock or a goat. That is blaspheme!"

Hearing a direct assault on Islam, the Sultan blew up in rage". Tie his hands and feet and drown him in the Ganga!"

But so sooner did the sepoys carry out this order than Kabir was seen floating on the surface without any fetter[1].

1. Kabir refers about this incident in his one 'Pada' in which he says : Janjeer bandhi kari khare kabir, Ganga ki lahar, meri tooti janjeer

[thrown into the Ganga with my body chained but the waves of the Ganga themselves snapped my fetters]

Seeing Kabir alive and sound in body and spirit, the Sultan thought the culprit might be versed in some magic art to release his body so soon. Then the Sultan ordered that he be burned alive. Again his hands and feet were tied and he was imprisoned in a hut which was set ablaze. But the hut was reduced to ashes and Kabir again emerged unscathed.

Now Sultan thought that he ought to be thrown before a mad elephant, for death, was the only consequence of the infidel's ego.

The order was complied with. The elephant was so furious that it was trying to crush its own shadow madly when Kabir was thrown before it. Then Kabir gazed at the pachyderm. All of a sudden the elephant ran away as though he was facing a king lion[1].

1. Kabir also refers about this incident in his following 'Pada'

Aahi mere thakur tumhara jor
Quazi bakibo hasti tor
Bhuja bandhi mila kari daryo
Hasti kopi moonda mahi maryo
Bhayo hasti cheesa Haree
Ya moorati ki hon baliharee

[Oh lord! I survive on your strength. Though I was thrown before a mad elephant at the Quazi's instigation, it ran away dashing its trunk on the ground out of fright. Blessed is thy form which made me survive]

This way Kabir remained invincible for even the Sultan. No harm could reach near him because he had the backing of his Lord Ram.

These events shouldn't be deemed as miracles because they symbolise the invincible strength of Kabir's inner convictions. He denounced all the dogmatic faiths that sought division of mankind. His was the voice of love for all beings.

He never cared for the cruditity of the language employed to blast away the superstitious and false divisions of society. Perhaps his illiteracy came as a strong weapon in his hand because he chose only those terms that were understood better by the masses sans any euphemistic cover of a flowery language. His attack was direct and hence more effective. He spared no one in his attack irrespective of the creed or caste he himself belonged to. His was the voice of truth. Despite his loving Ram he never spared the

Hindus and despite his being a born Muslim he dealt heavy blows at the Mullah and Quazis. He taught what all faiths teach in essence but since each faith has its declared custodians they change the thrust of each faith guided by their petty ego. Very rarely has the world witnessed a freer soul than the one that was housed in Kabir's body.

V. His Last Days

As has already been mentioned, Kabir was an old man when he confronted Sikandar Lodi. Going by the available records he might well have been in his nineties at that time. Yet though weaker in body he was firmer in lambasing the pseudo custodians of the Hindu and Muslim faihts. He always believed that faith can not be bound by regimentation. Communalism is not a faith because it has a parochial vision. The ultimate aim of every faith is to reveal the Supreme soul with in every soul. He taught the lesson of freedom of soul, liberty of the self to perceive the self fully and finally.

Nevertheless, he had to accept the limitations of age He believed that :

"Jo pahira so phatisee, naau dhara so jai", i.e., that which is mortal must perish. No matter what form the soul dons the cover has to perish the same way as the body rejects its clothes when they are torn.

He also realised that it was time he quitted his mortal coil. He was already in Kashi, a city known to ensure Moksha to the soul that sheds its mortal covers there. It was a prevalent belief which still exists among the traditional believers and hence their repairing to Kashi to die. This belief had led to various cruel methods of dying. Some even preferred taking 'Kashi-Karvat'. Perhaps this was the most religious method of committing suicide in the Medieval period. Is it a person, voluntarily willing to set his soul free from the cage of the body, would lie on a platform jutting out over the Ganga water in such a way that his head would be towards the river. Then he would be asked to change his side by the expert priest. At that very moment, amidst the chanting of shlokas, a heavy, sharp-edged iron blade would fall on the neck of the person lying on his side, hacking the head off to make it fall in the Ganga. This way the person willing to voluntarily die would die with the scene of Ganga's rippling waves in the holiest of holy city of Kashi secured in his eyes to ensure his soul's instant Moksha.

Despite all these cruel practice being very much in vogue during the times of Kabir he chose to die not in Kashi. Rebel to the conventions as he was, he thoroughly despised all such absurd beliefs about one's attaining Moksha if one died at Kashi. In sharp contradiction there was a small town called Maghahar where death was supposed to take one's soul to hell and hence it supposedly never received salvation.

Deeming his end to be nigh, Kabir declared henceforth his abode would be in Maghahar and not in Kashi. Having fought for his entire life against such senseless superstitious, he decided to fight against this superstition as well.

When Kabir's disciples heard about their mentor's this decision, they were aghast. Then Kabir explained to them :

Loga tum han mati ke bhora!
Jan Kashi tanu tajahi Kabira tau Ramahi kaun nihora?
Jo jan bhan bhagati kachhu jane
Takon acharaj kaho

Jaisen jal jalahi dhuri milayo,
Tyon dhuri milyo julaho
Kahe Kabir sunahu re loyee meram na bhoolyo koi
Kya Kashi kya Maghahar ookhar hridey Ram jo hoi

[Meaning : O people you all are not wise. If Kabir sheds his mortal coil in Kashi then wherefore he had been chanting the name of Ram all this while. In other words, death in Kashi might already ensure the final release of the soul; what in it would be the contribution of my chanting Lord Ram's name. If that guileless faith has any efficacy then by the grace of Lord Ram my soul would secure emancipation even after my dying at Maghahar. This is known to the men having discerning wisdom and they should not be surprised. It is like a drop of water conflumcing with the ocean sans its identity as a weaver or of any higher caste. Says Kabir that this basic fact shouldn't be missed. He who has Ram in his heart-for him it is immaterial whether he quits his mortal coil at Kashi or Maghahar]

So, sticking to his guns and not renouncing his campaign of hitting at the very base of all false presumptions having a pseudo religious sheens, Kabir, at last reached Maghahar.

Kabir's advent in Maghahar caused a great stir among the masses. All of a sudden the most despised place became a great source of attraction for the people. Almost a 'Mela' ensued there of unending duration. All came there with the aspiration of having Sant Kabir's Darshan. Kabir enlightened their souls as best as he could. People developed great faith in whatever Kabir taught. His 'Pada' and

'Saakhis' came to be sung with great verve and conviction. Kabir made Maghahar almost like another Kashi.

His 'Dohas' came to be known as Sakhee which is the corruption of the word 'Sakshee'. Now Sakshee literally means a witness who has watched an event with his own eyes. So in calling these 'Dohas' of Kabir Saakhee's the inherent meaning is that Kabir has witnessed it with his own eyes. Finally the day dawned when Kabir felt as though his soul was getting restless to meet the Ultimate Soul. So he called all his follows close to him. They came with a trepidaion in their hearts. Kabir asked them to keep quiet. Then he looked towards them with a steady gaze. All those who were present there felt a kind of very soothing light emerging from his eyes. Realising that their guide and mentor about to leave his mortal coil, one of them started singing :

"Jheeni-Jheeni beeni chadariya!"

While all were devotedly singing this famous 'Pada', Kabir breathed his last.

The Kabir-panthis record that some of them present there saw a divine beacon emanating from his body and going heavenwards. His soul had coalesced with the Supreme Being.

As the news of his death spread people came charging from all over the region. Soon a huge congregation of people surrounded his mortal body. Then arose a new controversy. How should his last rites be performed?

While the Hindus, led by Kashi Naresh(King of

Kashi) Veer Singh Ji, insisted upon Kabir be cremated in accordance with Hindu scriptures, the Muslims insisted that he be buried since he was born Muslim.

Tension arose as much as to make the two groups draw their daggers out of their scabbard. Ironically, what Kabir had fought for all his life appeared to have been negated by this controversy. It is claimed that before the fight could start, leaders of both the sides heard a kind of divine voice : "Don't Quarrel! First open the gate of the hut in which the body is kept".

When they rushed inside to the hut in which Baba's(Kabir's) body was kept, they were amazed to find no body there. Instead, there were lying some fresh flowers emanating an enchanting fragrance. Both the communities divided the flowers between themselves and performed the last rite in accordance with their religious beliefs.

Since then Maghahar has become almost a teertha for those who cherish the freedom of soul. Kabir Jayanti is celebrated there every year on Jyestha Poornima.

VI. Poem of Kabir

[His Dohas and Pada with their original text, its Romanised Versions and Hindi and English translation]

साखी या दोहा

आया था संसार मैं देषण को बहु रूप।
कहै कबीरा संत हौ, पड़ि गया नज़रि अनूप।

कबीर कहते हैं कि मैं इस संसार में अपनी अनेक वासनाओं से प्रेरित अनेक रूप देखने के लिए आया था। परन्तु हे संतो यहाँ पर गुरु कृपा से अनुपम रूप अर्थात् परमतत्व के दर्शन हो गए। इससे अनेक रूपों को देखने की अभिलाषा ही नहीं रह गई।।1 ।।

आसा एक जु राम की दूजी आस निरास।
पाँणी माँहे घर करैं ते भी मरै पियास।

आशा तो केवल राम की करनी चाहिए। बाकी सब आशाएँ व्यर्थ हैं । (अन्य देवताओं का आश्रय तो निरर्थक है।) आश्चर्य तो यह है कि जिसका निवास ही जल में है वह भी प्यासा ही है।।2 ।।

इक दिन ऐसा होगा सब सूँ पडै बिछोय।
राजा राणा छत्रपति, सावधान किन होय।

एक दिन व्यक्ति को सभी से बिछुड़ना पड़ेगा। इस निश्चित नियति को सोचकर राजा, राणा और छत्रपति सतर्क क्यों नहीं होते हैं(अर्थात वे विषय भोगों से विरक्त होकर ईश्वर भजन में क्यों नहीं लगते)।।3 ।।

अंषड़ियाँ झाँई पड़ी पंथ को निहारि निहारि।
जीभड़ियाँ छाला पड़्या राम पुकारि– पकारि ।

प्रियतम की बाट देखते–देखते आँखों में अँधेरा–सा छाने लगा है। इस जिह्वा पर भी राम को पुकारते–पुकारते छाले पड़ गए हैं अर्थात् ये दोनों अंग पीड़ित हो गए हैं परन्तु अभी तक भगवान से मिलन नहीं हुआ।।4 ।।

Saakhee or Dohas

Aayaa tha sansār me, deshan ko bahu roop |
Kahe Kabirā Sant hau, padi gayā nazari anoop ||

Says Kabir that I came into this world propelled by my passion to behold many comely forms. But, O Saints! The grace of my Guru made me behold the ultimate form which eliminated my desire to behold any other form ||1||

Āsā ek ju Ram kee dooji ās nirās |
Pānee manhi ghar karen, tey bhee maren piyās ||

One should pin one's hope for redemption only on Ram. Rest of the hopes only yield disappointment. What in amazing is that even the dewellers in water die of thirst ||2||

Ek din eisāhoyega, sab soon parhe bichhoya |
Rājā Rānā Chhatra pati, sāvdhan kin hoya ||

One day shall certainly dawn when each one will be separated by the rest. Deeming this as the ordained destiny for every one why don't the kings and emperors become more circumspect [and grow averse to sensual pleasures and devote themselves to worshipping the God]||3||

Akhariyā n jhā yee parhee, panth nihār-nihār |
Jeebhadiyan chhala padya, Ram pukār-pukār ||

Waiting for the beloved the eyes got clouded with darkness. Even the tongue developed blisters calling the name of Ram, [even the body organs have become afflicted] but Meeting with Lord has yet to take place ||4||

अकथ कहानी प्रेम की कछू कही न जाय।
गूँगे केरी सरकरा, खाई और मुस्काय।

कबीर कहते हैं कि प्रेम की कथा अकथनीय है। इसका वर्णन उसी प्रकार नहीं किया जा सकता जिस प्रकार गूँगा व्यक्ति शर्करा को खाकर आनंदित तो होता रहता है किन्तु उसकी मधुरता का वर्णन नहीं कर सकता।।5।।

आपनपौ न सराहिए, और न कहिये रंक।
नाँ जाँणौं किस बिरख तलि, कूड़ा होई करंक।

आत्मश्लाघ्या करना तथा दूसरों को तुच्छ समझना – दोनों ही मिथ्या अभिमान के चिह्न हैं। यह शरीर नश्वर एवं तुच्छ है। पता नहीं यह शरीर हड्डियों का ढेर मात्र बनकर किस वृक्ष के नीचे पड़ा रहेगा।।6।।

इस तन का दीवा करौं, बाती मेल्हूँ जीव।
लोही सीचौं तेल ज्यूँ , कब मुख देखौं पीव।

विरह की असह्य उत्कृष्टता में आत्मा कह रही है कि इस शरीर का दीपक बना लूँ और प्राण को उसकी बत्ती कर दूँ। इसे अपने शरीर के रक्त–रूपी तेल से सींचती रहूँ ताकि उस प्रकाश में प्रियतम का मुख शीध्र दिखाई दे जाए।।7।।

एक कनक अरु कांमनी, दोऊ अगनि की झाल।
देखें ही तन प्रज्जलै, परस्यां ह्वै पैमाल।

कामिनि और कंचन दोनों ही अग्नि की ज्वाला के समान हैं और ऐसी प्रबल एवं विचित्र हैं कि इनके देखने–भर से व्यक्ति का शरीर जलने लगता है, (अर्थात वासना से उत्तप्त हो जाता है।) इनके स्पर्श अर्थात् अधिकार और उपभोग से तो व्यक्ति बिल्कुल भस्म ही हो जाता है।।8।।

ऐसा कोई नां मिलै, निज धर देइ जराइ।
पंच लरिका पटिका करि, रहै राम ल्यौ लाइ।

हमें ऐसा कोई विरक्त और अपरिग्रही जीव नहीं मिला जो अपनी विषय

Akatha kahā nee prem kee, kachhu kahee nā jā ya|
Goonge keri sarkarā , khayi aur muskā ya||

Says Kabir that the tale of love is indescribable . It can't be told like a dumb, can't describe the sweetness of sugar and enjoys it ineffably ||5||

Apanā pau nā sarahiye, aur na kahiye rank |
Na jane kis birakhi tali, koorha hoi kharank ||

Praising the self and belittling the others – both betray a false sense of ego. This body is fey and negligible since no one knows beneath which tree it may die and dry in decay||6||

Is tan kā deevā karon, bā tee melhun jeeva |
Leenhee seechaun tel jyoon, kali sukh dekhon peeva ||

In the extreme agony of separation the soul laments that I'd make my whole body a lamp and life-breath its wick; I'd consume my body to shed light so that I may behold my beloved's face in that glow||7||

Ek kanak aru kamini, dunoo agine kee jhal |
Dekhen hee tan prajjalen, parasyan hvei pamaal ||

A beautiful woman's body and gold, both, emanate such flames of fire(passion) as to burn one merely on beholding them, and incinerate one to ashes at their very touch||8||

Eisā koyee nā mile, nija ghar deyi jarā i|
Panchoo larikā pataki kari, rahe Ram hyo lai||

I am yet to meet anyone totally averse to worldly achievements; who could burn his body and family achievements dispassionately in the fire of his intensity of

–वासनाओं एवं शारीरिक सम्पत्ति–रूपी घर को ज्ञान और प्रेम की आग से नष्ट कर दे तथा अपने काम–क्रोधादि पांचों लड़कों की उपेक्षा करता हुआ उन्हें पटक कर भगवान के ध्यान में मग्न रहे ।।9।।

ऐसी बांणी बोलिए मन का आपा खोइ।
अपना तन सीतल करै, औरन कौं सुख होइ।

मानव को अपना अहंकार छोड़कर ऐसी मधुर और विनम्र वाणी बोलनी चाहिए जिससे उसे स्वयं भी शीतलता हो ओर सुनने वालों को भी सुख मिले।।10।।

कबीर आप ठगाइए, और न ठगिये कोई।
आप ठग्याँ सुख ऊपजै, और ठग्याँ दुख होई।

कबीर कहते हैं कि स्वयं किसी से ठगे जाओ, दूसरों को मत ठगो। स्वयं के ठगे जाने से दुःख की अनुभूति होती है। ।।11।।

कबीर इस संसार में, धणै मिनष मतिहीणं।
राम नाम जांणै नहीं, आये टापा दीन।

कबीर कहते हैं कि इस विश्व में अनेक व्यक्ति मतिहीन एंव अज्ञानी हैं। उन्हें राम नाम का ज्ञान नहीं है। वे केवल अपने जीवन को व्यर्थ खोने और भटकने के लिए ही आये हैं।।12।।

कबीर कठिनाई खरी, सुमिरतां हरि नाम।
सूली ऊपरि नट विधा, गिरूँ त नाहीं ठाम।

भगवान के नाम–स्मरण में अनेक कठिनाइयाँ हैं। यह भी नट के सूली पर चढ़कर किए जाने वाले खेलों के समान है। इस सूली पर से गिरने पर जैसे नट के बचने की कोई आशा नहीं है, वैसे ही इस भक्ति–साधना से पथ–भ्रष्ट होने पर जीव के उत्थान का कोई मार्ग नहीं है।।13।।

कबीरा कहा गरबियौ, काल गहै कर केस।
नां जांणै कहाँ मारिसी, कै घरि कै परदेस।

love for God||9||

Eisee banee boliye, man kā apā khoye |
Apna tan sheetal kare, auran kon sukh hoye ||

Shedding one's arrogance one should always speak sweet and humble language which may not only provide coolness to oneself but also give happiness to others||10||

Kabira apa thagā iye, aur na thagiye koi |
Ā pa thagya sukh oopaje, aur thagyen dukh hoi ||

Kabir says never cheat anyone even though one may be cheated by others. For cheating others breeds sorrow while a kind of gratification ensues when one gets cheated by others||11||

Kabir is sansā r men, ghane minsh matiheen |
Rā m nā m jā ne nahen, ā ye tā pā deen ||

Kabir says that most of men in this world are devoid of wisdom; they don't seek the name of Ram and come to waste away their life in this world||12||

Kabir kathinā yee kharee, sumiratā m Hari nā m |
Sooli oopari nat vidya, giroon tau naheen thā m ||

Kabir says that there are innumerable difficulties in remembering God. It is akin to the trapeze-play performed over pointed bars and no hope for the one who falls down. [Meaning going astray on the path of god-realisation leaves no room for the soul's upliftment]||13||

Kabirā kahā garbiyā n, kā l gahe kar kesa|
Na jane kahan marisee, kai ghar kai pardesa||

कबीर कहते हैं कि इस क्षणभंगुर एवं अनिश्चित जीव पर क्या अभिमान करता है? मृत्यु ने जीव को बालों से पकड़ ही रखा है। पता नहीं काल उसे कहाँ मारेगा? उसके अपने घर पर ही अथवा परदेश में? (कहीं भी मार सकता है।)।।1 4।।

कबीर आपण राम कहि, औराँ राम कहाइ।
जिहि मुखि राम न ऊचरे, तिहि मुख फेरि कहाइ।

कबीर कहते हैं कि स्वंय रामनाम का उच्चारण करो तथा अन्य लोगों से भी कराओ। जिस मुख से रामनाम नहीं निकलता है उससे कहलाने की फिर फिर चेष्टा करो।।1 5।।

कबीर कहा गरबियौ, चाम पलेटे हड्ड।
हैबर ऊपरि छत्र सिरि, ते बी देबा खड्ड।

कबीर कहते हैं इस शरीर पर क्या गर्व करता है? यह चर्म से चिपटा हुआ हड्डियों का ढेर मात्र है। श्रेष्ठ एवं सुन्दर घोड़ों पर धारण करके चलने वाले शरीर भी एक दिन गड्ढे में गाड़ दिये जाएँगे।।1 6।।

कबीर कहा गरिबयौ, देही देखि सुरंग।
बीछड़ियाँ मिलिबौ नहीं, काँचली भुवंग।

रे मानव, इस सुन्दर शरीर को देखकर क्या अभिमान करता है। एक बार इससे बिछुड़ने पर फिर मिलन नहीं हो सकता है। छूटने के बाद यह शरीर पुनः उसी प्रकार नहीं प्राप्त होता है जैसे साँप अपनी केंचुली को जब एक बार छोड़ देता है तो फिर उसे नहीं ग्रहण कर सकता है।।1 7।।

कबीर कूता राम का, मुतिया मेरा नाँउँ।
गलै राम की जेवड़ी, जित खैंचे तित जाउँ।

कबीर कहते हैं कि मैं राम का कुत्ता हूँ। मेरा नाम मुतिया है। गले में राम की रस्सी पड़ी है, अर्थात, राम से बंधा हुआ हूँ। जिधर मुझे राम ले जाते हैं, उधर ही चला जाता हूँ।।1 8।।

Kabir says that it is useless to feel proud over this uncertain and fey course of life. Death ever holds one by hair and no one knows where one might breath one's last: at home or abroad||14||

Kabirā apan Rām kahi, auran Rām kahāi|
Jihi mukh Ram na oochare, tihi mukh nām kahāi||

Kabir exhorts all to chant Ram's name and make others do the same. If one fails to utter it, repeat the effort till one does so||15||

Kabir kahā garabiyo, chām palete hadd|
Haiber oopari chhata siri, te bee deba khudd||

Kabir says that one should not feel proud of one's body since it is nothing more than skeleton covered with skin. Even those who pompously ride stallions eventually fall in the chasm of death||16||

Kabir kahā garabiyo, dehi dekhi surang|
Beechhadiyan miliban naheen, Kanchalli bhujang||

O Man! Don't feel proud beholding your beautiful body! Once seperated you can never get it back like a snake can never get back its lost slough||17||

Kabir kootā Rām kā, Mutiya merā naun|
Gale Rām kee jevrhee, jita khenche tita jaun||

Kabir says that I am a pet dog of Ram and my name is Mutiya. His chain encircles my neck and I go where ever He draws me to ||18||

कबीर घास न निंदिए, जो पाऊँ तलि होइ।
उड़ि के परै जो आँखी में, खरी दुहेली होइ।

कबीर कहते हैं कि पैरों में पड़ी घास की भी अवज्ञा नहीं करनी चाहिए। किसी समय उसका भी महत्व होता है। अगर उसका कोई टुकड़ा भी आँख में पड़ जाता है तो अत्यन्त कष्टदायक होता है।।19।।

कबीर घोड़ा प्रेम का, चेतनि चढ़ि असवार।
ग्यांन षड़ग गहि काल सिरि, भली मचाई मार।

कबीर कहते हैं कि प्रेम (भक्ति) रूपी घोड़े पर चढ़कर तथा अपने हाथ में ज्ञान–रूपी तलवार लेकर इस चेतन रूपी घुड़सवार ने संसार के युद्ध–स्थल में काल–रूपी शत्रु के सिर पर गहरे आघात किए हैं।।20।।

कबीर जँत्र न बाजई, टूटि गए सब तार
जंत्र बिचारा क्या करे, चले बजावणहार।

कबीर कहते हैं कि मृत शरीर का यह बाजा अब नहीं बजता है। उसके तार सब टूट गए हैं। बेचारा यंत्र क्या करे? इसका तो बजाने वाला अर्थात् जीवात्मा ही इसे छोड़कर चला गया है।।21।।

कबीर तहाँ न जाइए, जहाँ कपट का हेत।
जालूँ कली कनीर की, तन रातौ मन सेत।

कबीर कहते हैं कि उस व्यक्ति के पास भी नहीं फटकना चाहिए जिसमें प्रेम का छल मात्र है, दिखावा है। जैसे कनेर की कली जो ऊपर से लाल है, परंतु भीतर से श्वेत है। जो व्यक्ति ऊपर से अनुरागमय प्रतीत होता है, परंतु अंदर से रागशून्य है, ऐसा व्यक्ति त्याज्य है।।22।।

कबीर तें काहे डरै, सिर परि हरि का हाथ।
हस्ती चढ़ि नहीं डोलिये, कूकर भसैं जु लाष।

कबीर, तुम क्यों डरते हो? तुम्हारे सिर पर भगवान का हाथ है। पर हाथी पर चढकर मत डोलो अन्यथा कुत्ते तुम्हारे पीछे भोंकते रहेंगे। (अर्थात्

Kabir ghās na nindiye, jan paun tali hoi|
Uri ken pare jo aankhi man, khari duheli hoi||

Kabir says that never despise even the grass that ever lies underfoot. At times it may also become important. Should a piece of it fall into the eyes, it rankles very painfully||19||

Kabir ghoda prem ka chetani chaddhi asawā r |
Myā n sharhag gahi kal sira, bhake machā yee rā r ||

Kabir says that riding the horse of devotion to God, holding the sword of wisdom in one hand, this concious horseman has been able to cast deadly wounds on the head of enemy-Time-in the battle field of the world||20||

Kabir jantra na bājayee, tooti gaye sab tā r |
Jantra bicharā kyā kare, chale bajā van-haar ||

Kabir says when the string(life breath) of the musical instrument(human body) is broken, the music stops because its Player has departed||21||

Kabir tanhā n na jayeeye, jahā n kapat ka heta |
Jaallon kali kaner kee, tan ratau man seta ||

Kabir says that shun that person whose love is deceitful: it shows like the outer redness of the flower of kaner though inwardly it is colourless||22||

Kabir toon kahe darei, sira par hari ka hā th |
Hasti chadhi nahin doleeye, koo-kar bhasam julaath ||

Why must you be afraid, O Kabir! The protecting head of God is over your head. Nevertheless, never strut in arrogance riding an elephant or you will be assailed by the barking dogs[i.e., shun arrogance or you shall be the object

अहंकारी और परिग्रही मत बनो, अन्यथा लोगों की ईर्ष्या के पात्र बन जाओगे।)।।23।।

कबीर थोड़ा जीवणां, माड़े बहुत मंड़ाण।
सबही ऊभा मेल्हि गया, राव रंक सुलितान।

कबीर कहते हैं कि थोड़े–से जीवन के लिए व्यक्ति ने बहुत से साज–समान एकत्र किए हैं। पर काल ने खड़े–खड़े ही राना, राव, रंक और बादशाह सभी को ग्रस लिया है।।24।।

कबीर देवल ढहि पड़्या ईंट भईं सैवार।
करि चेजारा सौं प्रीतिड़ी, ज्यूँ ढहै न दूजी बार।

यह मानव शरीर रूपी मन्दिर ढह गया है। इसकी ईंटें गलकर सैंवार (घास) में परिणित हो गई हैं। (इसके सब उपकरण ही मिट्टी में मिल गए हैं) कबीर कहते हैं कि इस मन्दिर के निर्माण करने वाले ईश्वर–रूपी निर्माता से प्रेम करो; ताकि इस मन्दिर को फिर कभी गिरना ही न पड़े अर्थात् जीव को जन्म–मरण से ही मुक्ति मिल जाए।।25।।

कबीर नौबति आपणीं, दिन दस लेहु बजाइ।
ए पुर पट्टन ए गली, बहुरि न देखे आइ।

रे जीव, सांसारिक सुखों की अपनी इस नौबत को दस दिन और बजा लो। उसके बाद तो तुम्हें यह नगर, यह शहर, ये गलियाँ देखने को मिलेंगी नहीं। (अर्थात् एक बार यह मानव जीवन मिल गया है, उसमें चाहे जितना अहंकारपूर्ण एवं भोगविलासमय जीवन व्यतीत करके इस सुयोग को नष्ट करो। फिर कभी तो यह सुयोग मिलने वाला नहीं है)।।26।।

कबीर पढ़िबो दूरि करि, पुस्तक देइ बहाइ।
बावन आखर सोधि करि, ररै ममैं चित लाइ।

कबीर कहते हैं कि भक्तिशून्य अध्ययन को दूर कर दो। केवल पुस्तकों में मत भटको, इनको बहा दो। बावन अक्षरों का शोधन करके उनका मूल

of others jealousy]||23||

Kabir ghoda jeevanam, mā de bahut madā n |
Sab hee oobha melhi gayā, rao, rank sultā n ||

Kabir says that even in this fey and transistory life one gathers lots of things affectionately. But whether it be a king or pauper, death grabs all in one swipe||24||

Kabir deval dhahi padya, eenten bhayeen sewar |
Kari chejā rā son preetahee, jyoon dhahi na dooji bar||

Kabir says that the human body like a temple of God which has collapsed with its all organs getting covered by wild grass and gone awaste [So concentrate on loving the Idol of God inside the temple and not its fey covering, the temple]||25||

Kabirā naubat ā panee, din das lehu bajā ya |
Ei pur pattan, ei gali, bahuri na dekhe ā ya ||

Kabir says : O Man! Proclaim your felicity loudly by beating the drum for a week or ten days. Then after, all of the towns, lanes etc., where you have lived shall go out of your reach and you can never visit them||26||

Kabira padhabo doori kari, pustak deyi bahā yi |
Bawan akhar sodhi kari, raraei mamaei chita lā yi ||

Kabir says that don't blindly comply with what your study says or your book reveals. Draw them(after reading) aside and then concentrate on the essence of all teachings : discard all 52 letters[1] and concentrate on 'Ra' and 'Ma' [i.e., 'Rama' is the only essence of everything in life]||27||

सार ढूँढ़ कर उसी में अपने चित्त को रमाओ – यह मूल सार केवल 'र' और 'म' है अर्थात् 'राम' है।।27।।

ऐसा कोई नां मिलै, जासूँ कहूँ निसंक।
जासूँ हिरदे की कहूँ , सो फिरि माड़ै कंक।

मुझे ऐसा कोई विवेकी तथा सच्चा हितैषी नहीं मिला, जिसके समक्ष पथ–प्रदर्शन की आकांक्षा और विश्वास के साथ अपने हृदय की उलझनों को बिना किसी संकोच के प्रकट कर सकूँ। जिस किसी से मैं अपने हृदय की बात कहता हूँ वही एक और उलझन पैदा कर देता है,साधना के किसी पाखण्ड में फंसा देता है।।28।।

ऐसा कोई नां मिलै, सब विधि देइ बताइ।
सुनि मंडल मैं पुरिष एक, ताहि रहै ल्यौ लाइ।

ऐसा कोई तत्त्वज्ञानी तथा साधनाविज्ञ गुरू नहीं मिला जो मुझे वह मार्ग दिखा देता, जिससे मैं उस शून्य गगन में निवास करने वाले परम–तत्त्व में ध्यान लगाये रहता।।29।।

ऐसा कोई नां मिले, हम कौं दे उपदेश।
भौसागर मैं डूबतां, कर गहि काढ़ै केस।

हमें ऐसा कोई गुरू नहीं मिला जो सच्चे तत्त्व ज्ञान का उपदेश देता और इस भवसागर में डूबते हुए हमें अपने हाथ में बाल पकड़कर निकाल लेता।।30।।

पांणी केरा पूसला, राख्या पवन सँवारि।
नाना बाणी बोलिया, जोति धरी करतारि।

कबीर कहते हैं कि यह शरीर पानी का बुलबुला है और प्राण–रूपी वायु के सहारे टिका हुआ है। यह पंच भूतों का जड़ संघात अनेक प्रकार से बोल रहा है। इसमें सृष्टि–कर्त्ता ने ज्ञान की ज्योति प्रतिष्ठित कर दी है। यही प्राणी का रहस्य है।।31।।

Eisa koi na milei, jasoon rahun nisanka |
Jaasoon hiradei kee kahon, so phir made kanka ||

Never could I get any real confidant before whom I could have opened my heart, all whom I met caused greater apprehension when I revealed even a part of my heart [All whom I met further confused me; never could any one provide me true relief]||28||

Eisā Koi nā milā, sab vidhi deyi batāyi |
Suni mandal men purish ek, tahi rehey lyo lāi ||

Never could I get any one who could lead me to the One Dwelling in all space and time[i.e., to the Ultimate Self, the Supreme Being]||29||

Eisā Koi no mila, hum ko dey upadesh|
Bhausāgar men doobtān, kara gahi kādhe kesh||

Never could I get any(such guru) who could have shown me the right way by his sermons and have pulled me out of this sea of mundane existence by grabbing my hair|30||

Panee kerā poosalā, rakhyā pavaṇ sanwāri |
Nānā bani bolya, joti khari kartāri ||

[Kabir says that] This body is like a bubble of water sustaining the form by the pressure of the life-breath. This dead assimilation of five elements utters in a variety of ways because the Creator has endowed it with light of knowledge which is the mystery of a being's existance||31||

1. The text refers to 52 letters which is the number of letters in Nagari script.

कबीर बन बन मैं फिरा, कारणि अपणैं रांम।
रांम सरीखे जन मिले, तिन सारे सबरे कॉम।

कबीर कहते हैं कि मैं ईश्वर–प्राप्ति के लिए वन–वन में भटकता रहा। परंतु जब मुझे राम–रूप भक्तजनों से साक्षात्कार हुआ तब उन्होंने मेरे सब काम सिद्ध कर दिए।।32।।

कबीर बादल प्रेम का, हम परी बरस्या आइ।
अंतरि भीगी आतमा, हरी भई बणराई।

प्रभु या गुरु के प्रेम एवं अनुग्रह का बादल हम पर बरस गया। उसके प्रेमरस से मेरी अन्तरात्मा भीग गई और मैं आनन्द से भर गया। इसी आनन्द से संपूर्ण 'बनराजि' भी हरी–भरी हो गई अर्थात् सारा विश्व चेतन एवं आनन्दमय प्रतीत होने लगा।।33।।

कबीर माया डाकणीं, सब किसही कौं खाइ।
दाँत उपाड़ौ पापणीं, जे संतौं नेड़ो जाइ।

कबीर कहते हैं कि यह माया डाइन है, यह सभी संसारी व्यक्तियों को खा जाती है। परंतु यदि यह पापिन सन्तों के पास जाएगी तो उसके दाँत उखाड़ दूँगा। (तात्पर्य यह है कि माया का विनाशकारी एवं विषैला प्रभाव सन्त पर नहीं होता।।34।।

कबीर माया पापणीं, हरि सूँ करैं हराम।
मुखि कड़ियाली कुमति की, कहण न देई राम।

कबीर कहते हैं कि यह माया पापिन है। जीवों को भगवान् से विमुख करती है उन पर दुर्मति की कढ़ी लगा देती है। इस प्रकार कभी भी उनसे राम–नाम का उच्चारण नहीं होने देती है।।35।।

कबीर माया मोहणीं, जैसी मीठी खाँड़।
सतगुरू की कृपा भई, नहीं तौ करती भाँड़।

Kabir ban-ban men phira, karani apne Rām |
Ram sareekhe jan mile, tin sare sabre kam ||

Kabir says that he kept on wandering jungles after jungles for God-realisation. It is only when I ment the devotees of Ram that my all missions were accomplished||32||

Kabir badal prem ka, hum pari barasaya āyi|
Antar bheegee atma, hari bhayee banarayi||

It is only when the Lord or the Guru's grace ladden clouds rained over me that my soul was gratified reviving all the vegetation of my conscious-self||33||

Kabir māyā dākinee, sab kisahee ko khāi|
Dānta uparho pāpanee, je santo nerho jai||

Kabir says that this māyā (illusion) is a witch which devours all mortal beings. But if this sinful existence dares go close to the saints and noble men it would have its teeth uprooted[i.e., maya loses its effect when it goes close to God-realised saints]||34||

Kabir māyā papanee, Hari soon kare harām|
Mukha karhiyali kumati ku, kahan na deyi Rām||

Kabir says that this sinful māyā makes the beings indifferent to God by chuitching their mouth with ignorance, to render them incapable of uttering Ram's name||35||

Kabir māyā mohanee jaise meeti khānda|
Satguru ki kirpa bhayee, nahee tau karatee bhanda||

Kabir says that this māyā is an enchantress which

कबीर कहते हैं कि यह माया मोहिनी है। शक्कर जैसी मीठी है। सद्गुरू की कृपा हो गई कि ज्ञान–वैराग्य जाग गया, अन्यथा तो यह माया मुझे भाण्ड (अर्थात् बहरूपिया एंव मिथ्या प्रशंसक) बनाकर ही छोड़ती अथवा हँसी का पात्र बना देती।।36।।

कबीर माया मोहणिं, मोहे जांण सुजांण।
भाग्यां ही छूटै नहीं, भरि–भरि मारै बांण।

कबीर कहते हैं कि यह माया मोहिनी है। यह ज्ञानी और बुद्धिमानों को भी मोहित कर लेती है। इसकी मोहिनी शक्ति से तो भाग कर अर्थात् इससे अलग रहने के प्रयास से इससे मुक्ति नहीं मिल सकती है क्योंकि यह पूरी शक्ति के विषय–रूपी बाण मारती है।।37।।

कबीर मारग अगम है, सब मुनिजन बैठे थाकि।
तहाँ कबीरा चलि गया, गहि सतगुरू की साषि।

ब्रह्म–प्राप्ति का मार्ग दुर्गम है। सब मुनि गण चलने से थक कर बीच में ही बैठ गए हैं। परंतु कबीर अपने गुरू की साक्षी से अर्थात् उनकी कृपा के बल पर वहाँ पहुँच गया है।।38।।

कबीर माला काठ की, कहि समझावै तोहि।
मन न फिरावै आपणाँ, कहा फिरावै मोहि।

कबीर कहते हैं– रे मानव, तुझे काठ की माला भी चेतावनी दे रही है। वह कहती है कि तू मन को तो संसार से फिराता नहीं है जिससे कल्याण हो सके,मुझे (माला के मनके) फिराने से क्या होता है?।।39।।

कबीर यह तन जात है, सकै तो लेहु बहोड़ि।
नागे हाथूँ ते गये, जिनकै लाखि करोड़ि।

कबीर कहते हैं कि यह शरीर जा रहा है। अगर सामर्थ्य हो तो इसको वापस फेर लो अर्थात् इसका भगवद्भक्ति के लिए सदुपयोग करो। जिन

appears sweet as sugar. But for my Guru's grace it would have also made me an impostor or bluffer babbling non-shine and becoming an object of ridicule||36||

Kabir māyā mohanee mohe jānā sujāna|
Bhagyān hee chhoote nahen, bhari-bhari māre bana||

Kabir says that this maya is such an enchantress as to confuse even the learned and wise. It is difficult to get redemption from it because it keeps on aiming at us with the powerful arrows inducing temptation to worldly pleasures||37||

Kabir mārage agam hai, sab muni jan baithje thāki|
Tahan Kabira chali gayā, gahi sat guru ki sāki||

The path towards God-realisation is very inaccessible making even the high sages and seers retire mid-way in sheer exhaustion. But Kabira with the help of the guru's grace could reach the destination||38||

Kabira mala kath ki, kahi samjhave tohi|
Man na phirāve apna, kaha phirāve mohi||

Kabir says : 'O Man this string of the wooden beads warns you every moment that instead of moving it, move your inner-self to observe it from all angles. Only then your welfare could be ensured and not by this listless movement of the string of the beads||39||

Kabir yaha tan jāt hai, sake to lehu bahori|
Nage ha thoon to gaye, jinke laakhi-karori||

Kabir says that every moment this body is getting consumed. If you have capacity, check its decay by devoting your attention to God. Else, even those who had billions

लोगों के पास लाखों और करोड़ों की सम्पत्ति थी,वे भी रीते हाथ रह गए हैं।।40।।

कबीर यहु घर प्रेम का, खाला का घर नाहिं।
सीस उतारै हाथि करि, सो पैठै घर मांहि।

कबीर कहते हैं कि यह घर प्रेम का है, अपनी मौसी का नहीं। यहाँ रोने–धोने या अनुनय–विनय से काम नहीं चलता।प्रेम के घर में वही प्रवेश कर सकता है, जो सिर उतार कर अपने हाथ पर रख लेता है, अर्थात् अपना अहं भगवान् को समर्पित कर देता है, प्रेम के लिए मृत्यु का वरण करता है।।41।।

कबीर संगति साध की, कदे न निरफल होइ।
चंदन होसी बाँवना, नींव न कहसी कोइ।

कबीर कहते हैं कि साधु की संगति कभी भी निष्फल नहीं जाती है। साधु बाहरी आकार–प्रकार में चाहे कितना ही छोटा प्रतीत होता हो, परंतु आभ्यन्तर शक्ति के कारण उसकी उपेक्षा नहीं हो सकती है। जैसे– चंदन का वृक्ष छोटा होने पर भी नीम नहीं कहला सकता है।।42।।

कबीर संगति साध की, बेगि करीजै जाइ।
दुरमति दूर गँवाइसी, देसी सुमति बताइ।

कबीर कहते हैं कि साधु की संगति करने में तत्परता दिखानी चाहिए। वह दुर्बुद्धि दूर करेगी और सुमति प्रदान करेगी।।43।।

कबीर सब सुख राम है, और दुखां की रासि।
सुर–नर–मुनियर असुर सब, पड़े काल की पासि।

कबीर कहते हैं कि केवल भगवान् एवं उनका स्मरण ही आनन्द–रूप तथा सुखों के हेतु हैं। अन्य सब कार्य तो दुःखों का समूह है दुःखों के हेतु हैं। देवता, मनुष्य, मुनिवर एवं असुर सभी मृत्यु के पाश में पड़े हुए हैं।।44।।

had to quit this world empty-handed||40||

Kabir yeh ghar prem ka khelā kā ghar nāhin|
Seesa utāre haathi kari, so paithe ghar māhin||

Kabir says that the abode of love is not your aunt's(mother's sister's) house where you could get entry by cajoling and crying. Here the entry is assured to only those who are capable of shedding their head(or ego) and offer it with their hands[to the beloved].||41||

Kabir sangate sādhu ki, kade na nirphal hoye|
Chandan hosi bavna, neemva na kahasi koya||

Kabir says that noble company never goes a waste. However small be a sandalwood tree it emits its fragrance more then emitted by even a big neem tree||42||

Kabir sangati sādhu ki, begi kareeje jāi|
Durmati door ganvaisee, desi sumati batāi||

Says Kabir that one should never delay in seeking a noble company which will remove ignorance and make one endowed with right kind of wisdom||43||

Kabir sab sukh Rām hai, aur dukhan ki rāsi|
Sur-nar-muniyar asur sab, padhe kal ki pāsi||

Opines Kabir that only devotion to God(Ram) is the mine of all happiness[in this mundane world]. The rest of the endeavours yield only sorrow since all gods, men, sages and even demons are bound by the noose of death.[And only devotion to God can redeem one from this bondage]||44||

कबीर यहु जग अंधला, जैसी अंधी गाइ।
बच्छा था सो मरि गया, अभी चांम चटाइ।

कबीर कहते हैं कि यह संसार अपनी वासनाओं में उसी प्रकार अंधा है जैसे स्नेह के मोह में गाय अंधी रहती है। अपने बच्चे के मर जाने के बाद गाय खड़ी–खड़ी मृत चर्म के कृत्रिम बछड़े को चाटती रहती है, वैसे ही यह जीव भी मोहवश सत्य को छोड़कर जगत्–रूप आभास से ही प्रेम करता रहता है।।45।।

कबीर सुमिरण सार है, और सकल जंजाल।
आदि अंति सब सोधिया, दूजा देखौं काल।

कबीर कहते हैं कि भगवान् का स्मरण ही सार वस्तु है। बाकी सब तो केवल झंझट है, बन्धन के हेतु हैं। मैं आदि–अन्त अर्थात् साधन एवं परिणाम पर अच्छी तरह विचार करके इस निष्कर्ष पर पहुँचा हूँ कि इसके अतिरिक्त दूसरे सब नाश के कारण हैं।।46।।

कबीर सूता क्या करै, गुण गोबिंद के गाइ।
तेरे सिर पर जम खड़्या, खरच कदे का खाइ।

जीव को चेतावनी देते हुए कबीर कहते हैं– रे जीव ! तू सोया हुआ क्या कर रहा है ? तेरे सिर पर काल खड़ा हुआ है और पता नहीं कब से वह तेरे ही खर्चे पर जी रहा है। तेरे अज्ञान के कारण ही यह जीवित है। तू भगवान् का स्मरण क्यों नहीं करता, ताकि तुझे इस काल से छुटकारा मिल जाय।।47।।

कबीर सोई दिन भला, जा दिन संत मिलाँहि।
अंक भरे भरि भेंटिया, पाप सरीरौं जाँहि।

कबीर कहते हैं कि वही दिन अच्छा है जिस दिन संत लोग मिलते हैं। उनके गले से गले मिलने से शरीर के सम्पूर्ण पाप नष्ट हो जाते हैं।।48।।

Kabir yahu jag āndhala, jaisee andhee gā ye|
Bacchha-thā so mare gayā, abbee chā m chatā ya||

Kabir says that this mortal life, blended by a variety of passion, is akin to a blind cow which keeps on licking its beloved heifer's body even after the latter's death||45||

Kabir sumiran sar hai, aur sakal janjā l|
Aadi anti sab sodhiya, dooja dekhon kā l||

Says Kabir that the only essence of this mortal world is remembrance of God, for other pursuits only create confusion and bondage. Having weighed all pro's and con's his considered opinion is that all the rest lead to the ways of destruction||46||

Kabir soota kyā kare, guna Govinda ki gā yi|
Tere sir par Jam khadyā, kharach kadi ka khayi||

Warning the beings Kabir says that don't waste time in slumber and worship the Ultimate. The sword of the Death-god is hanging over your head and your ignorance is paying for this arrangement. Remove it and get redemption from Time through remembering God||47||

Kabir soye din bhalā, ja din sant milā hi|
Ank bhare bhari bhentiya, pap sareeron jā hi||

Kabir says that only that day is ausicious when one gets noble persons and saints. By embracing them almost all sins of the body get dissolved into naught||48||

कबीर सोइ सूरिमां मन सूँ मांड़ै झूझ।
पंच पयादा पाड़ि ले, दूरि करै सब दूज।

कबीर कहते हैं कि सच्चा शूरवीर वही है जो वासनापूर्ण मन से युद्ध करके उसके शब्द, स्पर्श, रूप–रस और गन्ध अथवा ज्ञानेन्द्रियों रूपी उसके पाँचों पैदल सैनिकों को भगा देता है और इस प्रकार द्वैत–भाव को नष्ट करने में सफल हो जाता है।।49।।

कबीर सो धन संचिये, जो आगै कूँ होई।
सीस चढ़ाएँ पोटली, ले जात न देख्या कोइ।

कबीर कहते हैं कि जो धन–द्रव्य परलोक के लिए हो सके उसका ही संचय करना चाहिए। वह धन तो ज्ञान और प्रेम ही है। लोग सांसारिक धन–संचय में जुटे हुए हैं। परंतु हमने तो मर जाने वाले किसी भी व्यक्ति के सिर पर इस धन की पोटली को नहीं देखा है।।50।।

कबीर हसणाँ दूरि करि, करि रोवण सौं चित्त।
बिन रोयाँ क्यूँ पाइए, प्रेम पियारा मित्त।

कबीर कहते हैं कि हँसना छोड़कर रोने में मन लगाओ, व्यथा में तन्मय हो जाओ। बिना रोये ही प्यारा प्रेमी और मित्र मिलते हैं ?।।51।।

कबीर हरि की भगति बिन, ध्रिग जीवण संसार।
धूँवा केरा धौलहर, जात न लागै बार।

कबीर कहते हैं कि भक्ति के बिना संसार में यह जीवन ही धिक्कार–योग्य है। यह जीवन धूप या बादलों का महल है। इसको नष्ट होते देर नहीं लगती।।52।।

कबीर हरि रस यौं पिया, बाकी रही न थाकि।
पाका कलस कुंभार (कुम्हार) का,बहुरि न चढ़ई चाकि।

कबीर ने भगवान् के साक्षात्कार एवं प्रेम का रस इस प्रकार और इतना पी

Kabir soyee soorama, man soon madhe jhoojha|
Pancha payada pā rhi le, doori pare sab doojha||

Says Kabir that the real valiant is one who can fight against its own mind steeped in a variety of passions to rout the five soldier of the senses and remove all sense of duality||49||

Kabir so dhan sanchiye, jo āge koon hoi|
Seesa chadhayen potali, le jat na dekhya koi||

Kabir says that teasure is that wealth which may prove useful in the next life as well. That wealth is of knowledge and love. Even then people are engrossed in amassing material wealth. Yet no one has been seen carrying it to the next world over one's head after death||50||

Kabir hasanā doori kari, kari rovan son chitta|
Bin royā n kyoon paiyee, prem piyā rā mitta||

Kabir says that stop laughing and devote your mind to crying since without shedding tears no one can get one's beloved||51||

Kabir Hari ki bhagati bin, dhriga jeevan sansā r|
Dhoovan kera dhaulhar, jat na lā ge bā r||

Kabir says that Jie upon that life that is devoid of devotion[to God] since this mortal life is as fey as a palace of clouds or smoke dissipating in no time||52||

Kabir hari ras yon piya, baqee rahee no thaki|
Paka kalash kumbhar ka, bahuri no chadhai chaki||

Kabir has imbibed the elixir of God-realisation as much as to get totally refreshed from the exhaustion of this

लिया है कि अब उसकी सांसारिक यात्रा की थकान बिल्कुल दूर हो गई है। भक्त कबीर भगवान् रूपी कुम्भकार का घड़ा है। उनके अनुग्रह एवं ज्ञान से उसका शरीर रूपी घट पक गया है, इसलिए संसार के आवागमन रूपी चाक पर उसे फिर नहीं चढ़ना है। वह इसी जन्म में मुक्त हो गया है। ।53।।

कस्तूरी कुंडलि बसै, मृग ढूँढ़ै बन मांहि।
ऐसैं घटि घटि रांम है, दुनियाँ देखै नांहि।

मृग की नाभि में कस्तूरी रहती है। वह उसकी सुगन्ध से अभिभूत होकर उसे प्राप्त करने के लिए वन–वन में ढूँढ़ता फिरता है, वैसे आनन्द–स्वरूप भगवान् प्रत्येक के अन्त:करण में निवास करते हैं। जीव उस आनन्द के आभास से मुग्ध होकर उसे पूर्ण रूप से प्राप्त करने की इच्छा से विभिन्न साधनाओं में भटकता है।।54।।

कहा कियौ हम आइ करि, कहा कहैंगे जाइ।
इत के भए न उतीके, चाले मूल गँवाइ।

मैंने मानव– शरीर प्राप्त करके क्या किया? वहाँ जाकर ईश्वर के समक्ष क्या जवाब दूँगा? न इस लोक का आनन्द ही ले सका और न परलोक ही सुधार सका (इस प्रकार दोनों ओर से पतित हो गया हूँ।) अपनी ज्ञान, प्रेम और पुण्य की जो मूल निधि थी, वह भी मैंने गँवा दी है।।55।।

कागद केरी नाँव री, पांणी केरी गंग।
कहै कबीर कैसे तिरूँ, पंच कुसंगी संग।

कबीर कहते हैं कि यह शरीर कागज की नौका है और यह संसार मायामोह के जल से भरी हुई गंगा है। इस जीवन–यात्रा में मेरे साथ काम–क्रोधादिक पाँच दुर्जन साथी हैं। ऐसी अवस्था में इस संसार–रूपी गंगा से कैसे पार उतर सकूँगा?।।56।।

काजल केरी कोठड़ी, काजल ही का कोट।
बलिहारी ता दास की, जे रहै रांम की ओट।

mortal journey. He has become almost an earthen pot made by the Supreme Potter full of this elixir, as much mature in his understanding as to get away from the rut repeatedly moving over the Potter's wheel[i.e., from the cycle of births and deaths]||53||

Kasturi kundali basayi, mriga dhoondhe ban manhi|
Eisen ghati-ghati Ram hai, duniya dekha nahi||

Like a deer which wanders all over the jungle to get to the source of the musk-pod through it remains hidden in its navel region, man roams about all over the world to seek Ram(God) outside but He remains hidden in his ownself||54||

Kahā kiyā hum ayi kari, kahā kahenge jāyi|
Ita ke bhaye na uteeke, chāle moola ganvayi||

What did I do gaining this mortal coil? What would I say before the Maker on going back? Neither I could enjoy pleasures of this world nor could I improve my lot in th next. The worst part is that in this process I have also lost my innate treasure of knowledge and capacity to love. Now I return empty handed||55||

Kagad keri naav ree, paani keri gang|
Kahe kabir kaise tiroon, pāncha kusangi sang||

Kabir says that this body is like a paper-boat floating over the Ganga full of water with five co-travellers being five sensual perceptions of high sensitivity. How would I ever succeed in reaching the other shore?||56||

Kājal keri kothāri, kājal hee ka kot|
Balihari ta dās ke, je rahe Ram ki ot||

The whole world is a cell of black-soot(vices) which stands

यह जगत् काजल की कोठरी है,अर्थात् अज्ञान की कालिमा का स्थान है। इसका संरक्षण भी अज्ञान की चहारदीवारी द्वारा ही सम्भव है। उस भक्त को धन्य है जिसने भगवान् की शरण ले ली है। इनसे उस पर संसार की कालिमा का कोई असर ही नहीं होता।।57।।

काजल केरी कोठरी, मसि के कर्म कपाट।
पांहनि बोई पृथमीं, पंडित पाड़ी बाट।

बुतपरस्त या पंडित का यह संसार काजल की कोठरी है और उसके कर्म–रूपी स्याही के किवाड़ लगे हुए हैं। उसने चारों ओर पृथ्वी को पाषाण मूर्तियों से बो सा रखा है। इस प्रकार पंडित संसार पर डाका डाल रहा है।।58।।

काजी मुलां भरमियां, चल्या दुनीं कै साथि।
दिल थैं दींन बिसारिया, करद लई जब हाथि।

जब काजी और मौलवी ने जीव–हत्या के लिए अपने हाथ में छुरी पकड़ी, उसी समय से वे भ्रमित होकर धर्म के मार्ग से भटक गए हैं और दुनिया के साथ चलने लगे हैं। उन्होंने उसी समय से अपने धर्म को हृदय से भुला दिया है।।59।।

काबा फिर कासी भया, राम हुँ भया रहीम।
मौट (मौठ) चून मैदा भया, बैठि कबीरा जीम।

सम्प्रदायवादी आग्रहों का परित्याग करने, समन्वय के मध्यम मार्ग को अपनाने पर काबा काशी हो गया है राम रहीम बन गए हैं। क्योंकि अब भेद का ज्ञान कराने वाली उपाधि मूलतत्व में समाहित हो गई है। भेदों का घोटा चून अब पिस कर मैदा बन गया है। कबीर तू इस मैदा का भोजन कर।।60।।

केसौं कहा बिगाड़िया, जो मूँडै सौ बार।
मन कौं काहे न मूँडिए, जामैं विषै बिकार।

कबीर कहते हैं कि इन बालों ने क्या बिगाड़ा है कि इनको सैकड़ों बार मुँडाते हो। इस मन को क्यों नहीं मुँडाते हो जिसमें अनेक विषय–वासनाएँ

protected only in the fortress of ignorance. But blessed is that devotee who could seek shelter under God's(Ram's) grace to stay away from that filthy negrescence||57||

Kājal keni kothari masi ke karm kapāt|
Pahin boyee prithamee, pundit padhee bāt||

This world of icon worshippers or orthodox pundits is black cell of ignorance having the doors bearing the mark of destiny written with the black ink of deeds. These image worshippers have almost covered the whole earth with stone idols and ensuring no escape for the being the pundits are merrily plundering this world||58||

Kazi Mullan bhramiyan, chalya dunee ke sāthi|
Dil then deen bisariya, karad layee jabihathi||58||

When the Quazi and Maulvi took the knife in hand to butcher beings, they deviated from the righteous path. Now they follow the world and not the essence of their faith||59||

Kābā phir kāshi bhaya, Rāmuha bhaya Raheem|
Mauth choon maida bhāyā, baithi Kabeera jeem||

The Kaaba and Kashi, ram and Raheem lost their distinction for the one who could go to the soul of the two faiths. When the grains of faith distinction are grounded so fine as to become homogenous soft maida[1] they have the same taste and Kabir is merrily enjoying his food made of this maida.||60||

Keson kahā bigariya, jo moonday sau bār |
Man kon kahe na moondiye, ja men vishey vikār ||

Kabir says what harm the (head) hair has brought to you so that you shave them off, hundreds of times? Why don't you prune off the passions and lust that keep on

एवं उनके विकार भरे पड़े हैं।।61।।

खरी कसौटी रांम की, खोटा टिकै न कोइ।
रांम कसौटी सो टिकै,जौ जीवन्मृत होइ।

भगवान् अर्थात् भक्ति और ज्ञान की कसौटी खरी है, इस पर नकली व्यक्ति नहीं टिक सकता है। जो इस कसौटी पर खरा उतरता है, वह वास्तव में जीवन्मृत हो जाता है।।62।।

गुरू गोबिन्द तौ एक हैं, दूजा यहु आकार।
आप मेट जीवत मरै, तौ पावै करतार।

गुरू और गोविन्द दोनों एक ही हैं। इनका केवल आकार अर्थात् उपाधि ही भिन्न–भिन्न है। जो शिष्य अपने अहं को मिटाकर जीवित अवस्था में अर्थात् शरीर के रहते ही विषय–वासनाओं की आसक्ति छोड़ने के कारण उनके लिए मरा–सा हो जाता है, वही वास्तव में ईश्वर का साक्षात्कार कर सकता है।।63।।

गुरू गोविन्द दोऊ खड़े, काके लागौं पाय।
बलिहारी गुरू आपणै, गोविन्द दियो बताय।

कबीर कहते हैं कि यदि गुरू और गोविन्द (ईश्वर) दोनों मेरे सामने आजाएं तो पहले मैं गुरू के चरणों पर लगूँगा जिनकी कृपा से मुझे ईश्वर को पहिचानने की क्षमता मिल पाई।।64।।

ग्यान प्रकास्या गुरू मिल्या, सो जिनि बीसरि जाइ।
जब गोविन्द कृपा करी, तब गुरू मिलिया आइ।

रे मानव, जब गुरू मिले तब ज्ञान का प्रकाश हुआ है। अब उस ज्ञान को भूल मत जाना।(अन्यथा तुझे फिर उसी संसारचक्र में भटकना होगा) राम की कृपा हुई तब तो गुरू आकर मिले।।65।।

sprouting on your mind? || 61 ||

Kharee kasauti Rām ki, khota tikey na koy |
Rām kasauti jo tikey, jau jeevan-mrita hoya ||

The touchstone of Ram(God) is so true that the false can't withstand the test. And he who passes this test with flying colors transcends the limit of death and life. || 62||

Guru Govind tau ek hain, dooja yahu ākār |
Āpa meta jeevat marei, tan pāve kartar ||

God and the Guru have no difference; only their outer form is different. The disciple who in his life-time eliminates his self for various sensuous attachments and verily becomes dead becomes dead for them really realises God(and hence Guru for he is able to see through the difference). ||63||

Guru Govinda donoo khade kāke lagoon pānya|
Balihari Guru āpne, Govinda diyo batāya ||

Says Kabir that if he happens to meet both the Guru and God simultaneously he would first show his grateful reverence to the Guru who could develop the discernment in him to recognize God || 64||

Gyān prakāsyā Guru milā, so jini beesari jayi |
Jab Govinda kripa kari, tab guru miliya āyi ||

O Man! Enlightenment of knowledge dawned upon you when God shed grace upon you and only then you could meet you're your mentor, the Guru. Don't let this enlightenment be dissipated.(i.e. One gets one's Guru only when the providence wills so)||65||

---

1. The most reined flour of wheat grains.

चंदन भागां गुण करै, जैसे चोपीपंन।
दोउ जन भागा नां मिलै, मुकताहल अरू मंन।

चन्दन के टुकड़े करने पर उनमें से सुगन्ध निकलती है, और फैलती है, जैसे चोआ का लेप अथवा मंजीठ के पत्ते सुगन्ध देते हैं। पर मोती और मन ये दो वस्तुएँ विभक्त होने पर पुनः नहीं मिलती हैं और न ही इनके गुण में वृद्धि होती है।।66।।

चकवी बिछुटी रैणि की, आइ मिलि परभाति।
जे जन बिछुटे राम सूँ, ते दिन मिलैं न राति।

चकवी अपने पति से रात में बिछुड़ जाती है तो प्रातः काल आकर मिल लेती है। पर जो जीव भगवान् से बिछुड़ गए हैं उनका मिलन न रात में होता है और न दिन में (जीवन भर नहीं होता है)।।67।।

चारयूँ बेद पढ़ाइ करि, हरि सूँ न लाया हेत।
बालि कबीरा ले गया, पंडित ढूँढे खेत।

चारों वेदों को पढ़ाने पर भी पंडित वेदों के अध्येता में भगवान् के प्रति प्रेम उत्पन्न नहीं कर पाया। (अथवा चारों वेदों का वक्ता होने पर भी उसमें भगवान् के प्रति प्रेम नहीं जागा।) प्रेम– रस व ज्ञान रूपी अन्न से भरी हुई बाल तो कबीर ले गया और तथाकथित पंडित सार–शून्य शब्दों के खेत को ही ढूँढ़ता रहा।।68।।

जब गण कूँ गाहक मिलै, तब गुण लाख बिकाइ।
जब गुण कौ गाहक नहीं, तब कौड़ी बदलै जाइ।

गुण का ग्राहक मिलने पर ही गुण का मूल्य होता है। उस समय वह वस्तु लाखों में बिक जाती है। अगर गुण–ग्राहक का ही अभाव है तो वस्तु कौड़ियों के मूल्य में चली जाती है।।69।।

Chandan bhagan guna kare, jaise chopeepann|
Douoo jan bhagan na mile, mukta hal or mann||

The more a piece of sandalwood is divided the more it emits its fragrance, so is also true with the madder plant and the ointment made from four perfumes viz sandal, a gallodhum, saffron and musk. But when either a pearl or a heart is broken, neither they can again be united nor their innate qualities multiply||66||

Chakavee bichhutee raini ki, ayi mile par bhāti|
Je jan bichute Rām sau tey din milen na rati||

The female ruddy goose gets again united in day time. But those who are seperated from Ram neither in day nor in night can again be united[i.e., they are never united with their Lord]||67||

Charyoon Veda padhai kari, Hari soon na laya heta|
Bali Kabeer ley gaya, Pandit dhoondhey kheta||

Despite being learned in the four Vedas the Pundit couldn't develop love for God. It is because the essence of the love plant has been taken away by Kabir and the Pundit was left with the juiceless remains of that plant, though in vain he kept on searching it in the entire field.||68||

Jab guna koon gāhak miley, tah guna lakh bikāya|
Jab guna kau gahak naheen, tab kauree badle jāya||

When the qualities meet their connoisseurs their value is truly realised and they are sold in high price. In case they don't get their true connoisseurs they get sold for a pittance||69||

जहाँ न चीटीं चढ़ि सकै, राई ना ठहराइ।
मन पवन का गमि नहीं, तहाँ पहुँचे जाइ।

जो स्थान इतना दुर्गम है कि चींटी भी नही चढ़ सकती है, जो इतना ,सूक्ष्म है कि वहाँ राई तक के लिए स्थान नहीं है, और जहाँ मन और प्राण तक की गति नहीं है, कबीर उसी पद को पहुँच गए हैं।।70।।

जाका गुरु भी अंधला, चेला खरा निरंध।
अंधे अंधा ठेलिया, दुन्युं कूप पडंत।

जिसका गुरु अंधा है अर्थात अज्ञानी है, और जो शिष्य पूर्णतः अंधा है (उसका अंधा का सा व्यवहार होता है।) अधां अंधे को ठेलता है और दोनों कुएँ में गिर जाते हैं। अर्थात मार्ग और लक्ष्य को न जानने के कारण वे एक – दूसरे का ठेलते चलते है और अंत में विषय–वासना रुपी कुएँ में गिर कर दोनों नष्ट हो जाते हैं।।71।।

जाकै दिल में हरि वसै, सो नर कलपे कांइ।
एकै लहरि समंद की दुख दलिद्र सब जाइ।

जिस ह्रदय में भगवान का निवास है, अर्थात जिसे अपने ह्रदय में ईश्वर पर पूर्ण विश्वास है, उसे पछताने और दुःख भोगने की क्या आवश्यकता है? भगवान के अनुग्रह रूपी समुद्र की एक लहर मात्र से उसके सम्पूर्ण दारिद्य और दुःख समाप्त हो जाते हैं।।72।।

जाकै मुह माथा नही, नाही रूप अरूप।
पुहूप बास थै पातला ऐसा तत अनूप।

जीवात्मा के वास्तविक पति ब्रह्मा के न मुख है, न सिर है, न रुप है और न रेख। उसको रूपवान या रूप – रहित भी नहीं कहा जा सकता है। वह पुष्प की गंध से भी अत्यन्त क्षीण है अर्थात केवल अनुभूति–गम्य है। भगवान ऐसी अनुपम तत्त्व वस्तु है।।73।।

Jahā n na cheentee chadhi sake, rayee na thaharā ya|
Man pavan ka gami naheen, tahan pahunche jā ye||

The place so inaccessible that where not even an ant can reach or the mustard grain can't accommodated has been attained by Kabir. It is the place where even mind can't reach[That is, Kabir's flight of imagination reaches the place inaccessible to even an ordinary mind or any physical being; hence his observation are unique]||70||

Jaka Guru bhee andhala, chela khara nirandh|
Andhi andhā thelia, dunyoo koop parant||

He who is blind and his guru is also ignorant eventually falls in the well of ignorance propelled by his guru who also falls in that well. When a blind guides a blind this is the obvious consequence||71||

Jā ke dil men Hari basen, so nar kakpe kā ya|
Ekei lahar samanda ki, dukh dalidra sab jā ye||

He who has in his heart the abode of his chosen God need not fret and fume in frustration for any thing. Just one wave of the grace of the kind God is enough to eliminate all affliction and privations of the devotee||72||

Jake munh mā tha nahin, naheen roop aroop|
Puhup bas the pā tala, eisa tata anoop||

The real master of the soul has neither any form nor any physique, yet it can't be held to be attributeless. Even then it is subtler than the fragrance of a flower and is realisable only by feeling. Such are the incomparable qualities of God||73||

जाकौ जेता निरमया, ताकौं तेता होइ।
रती धटै न तिल बढै, जौ सिर कुट्टे कोइ।

जिसके लिए भगवान ने जितना भोग रचा है, उसको उतना ही प्राप्त होगा। उसमें तनिक भी परिवर्तन सम्भव नहीं है, चाहे कोई कितना भी प्रयत्न करे।।74।।

जिनके नौबति बाजती, मैंगल बंधते बारि।
एकै हरि के नाँव बिन, गए जनम सब हारि।

जिनके द्वार पर नौबत बजती थी और मस्त हाथी बँधते थे, केवल एक भगवान के नाम–स्मरण के अभाव में उनका सम्पूर्ण जीवन ही व्यर्थ हो गया।।75।।

जिहिं धट में संस बसैं, तिहिं धटि राम न जोइ।
राम सनेही दास बिचि तिणां न संचर होइ।

जिस अंत: करण में संशय अर्थात जीव एवं ब्रह्मा के अद्वैत अथवा भक्त और भगवान के ऐक्य में निष्ठा का अभाव या संदेह रहता है, उस अन्त: करण को भगवान राम का वास्तविक साक्षात्कार नहीं हो पाता है। भगवान राम एवं उनके स्नेही भक्तों के बीच में तृण मात्र का प्रवेश भी सम्भव नहीं है।।76।।

जिहिं घरि साध न पूजिये, हरि की सेवा नांहि।
ते घर मड़हट सारषै, भूत बसै तिन माँहि।

जिन घरों में साधु की पूजा और भगवान की उपासना नहीं है, वे घर शमशान के समान हैं। उनमें भूत रहते हैं। ।77।।

जिहि धट प्रीति न प्रेम रस, पुनि रसना नही राम।
ते नर इस संसार में, उपजि भये बेकाम।

कबीर कहते हैं कि जिनके हृदय में प्रेम का रस भरा हुआ नहीं है, जिसकी

Jāko jeta niramayā, takon tetā hoya|
Rati ghatei na til badhey, jau sira kootey koya||

One gets what one is destined for by God. Everyone's destiny is immutable no matter how valiantly one tries to alter it. One gets what God has destined for him, not a wee-bit less or more||74||

Jinkey naubat bājati, mangal bandhtey bāri|
Ekei Hari ke nava bin, gaye janam sab hāri||

They who had at their gates kettle drums beaten to herald their authority and the elephants strutting found their life going a waste when they failed to chant the name of God||75||

Jihi ghat men sansau base, tihi ghat Ram na joi|
Rām sanehi das bichi, tinā na sanchar hoi||

Those whose hearts have doubts can never realise God. Between god and his devotees there is no room even for a peck of straw[let alone doubt][unless there is derect communion between the devotee and his Lord, realisation is not possible]||76||

Jihi ghari sadha na pooyiye, Hari ki sewā nahin|
Tey ghar marghat sārashe, bhoot basey tin māhin||

Those houses where in the noble men are not respected and God is not worshipped are verily like crematoria where only ghosts dwell||77||

Jihi ghat preeti na prem ras, puni rasana nahin Rām|
Tey nar is sansar men, upaji bhaye bekām||

Says Kabir that futile is the berth of those beings whose hearts are not replete with love and whose tongues

जीभ पर राम का नाम है, उन प्राणियों का उस संसार में जन्म लेना भी व्यर्थ हो गया है।।78।।

जैसी मुख ते नीकसै, तैसी चालै चाल।
पारब्रह्म नेड़ा रहै, पल मैं करै निहाल।

जिन सिद्धांतों की बात व्यक्ति के मुख से निकलती है, अगर उन्हीं के अनुसार वह जीवन–यापन करे तो वह परब्रह्म के निकट आ जाता है। भगवान उस व्यक्ति को पल–भर में निहाल कर देते हैं।।79।।

ज्यों गूँगे के सैन का गूँगा ही पहचान।
त्यों ग्यानी के सुक्ख को ज्ञानी होय सो जान।

कबीर कहते हैं कि जिस प्रकार गूँगे के संकेत को कोई दूसरा गूँगा ही जान सकता है उसी प्रकार तत्वज्ञानी (आत्मा–परमात्मा के सम्बन्ध के वास्तविक ज्ञाता) के आनन्द को केवल ज्ञानी ही समझ सकता है।।80।।

जौ राउँ तौ बल घटै, हँसैं तौ राम रिसाइ।
मन ही माँही विसूरणा, ज्यूँ धुण काठहिं खाइ।

अगर रोता हूँ तो प्रेम की शक्ति कम होती है और अगर हँसता हूँ (अर्थात् विषयों में अनुरक्त होता हूँ अथवा व्यथा पर हँस लेता हूँ) तो व्यथा के कम हो जाने से भगवान् रुष्ट हो जाते हैं। इसलिए अन्तःकरण में इस प्रकार खोखला होता रहूँ जैसे दीमक के खाने से काठ होता रहता है।।81।।

ज्यूँ नैनूँ मैं पूतली, त्यूँ खालिक घट माँहि।
मुरिख लोग न जाँणहीं, बाहरि ढूँढण जाँहि।

जिस प्रकार नेत्रों में पुतली है वैसे ही भगवान सम्पूर्ण विश्व में व्याप्त है। परन्तु अज्ञानी व्यक्तियों को इसका ज्ञान नहीं है, अतः वे उस परमतत्व को अपने से बाहर खोजते रहते हैं।।82।।

don't chant Ram's name||78||

Jaisee mukh tey neekasey, taisee chā le chal|
Paarbhramha nerha rahe, pal men kare nihal||

One who lives and talks in strict adherence to one's convictions comes closer to Lord Supreme (as he develops divine power). God endows all felicity to such persons in no time.[i.e., there should be no difference in one's precepts and practice]||79||

Jyon goonge ke saina ko, goonga hee pahichā n|
Tyon gyā ni ke sukkha ko, gyā ni hoi so jā n||

Says Kabir that like a dumb's gestures are understandable only for a dumb so also the happiness of the wise is realisable only by the wise||80||

Jau rouoon tau bal ghate, hansau tau Rā m risā ya|
Man hee manhi bisoorana, jyoon ghun kā thahi khā ya||

If I weep the potency of my love gets reduced and if I laugh[i.e., gets drawn towards worldly enjoyments] owing to the lessening of my agony due to separation from the Lord, the lord gets displeased. Hence it is best to lament only inwardly so that my agony may make me hollow like the termite that nibbles at and makes a wood piece hollow||81||

Jyoon nainoon men pootali, tyoon khliq ghat manhi|
Moorikha log na janahin, bā har dhoodhan jā nhi||

Lord reposes in the entire world like the eye-ball in the eye. The ignorant, however, have no idea about it and they search the ultimate out of their self||82||

झूटे कौ झूठां मिलै, दूणँ बधँ सनेह।

झूठे कूँ साचा मिलै तब ही टूटै नेह।

झूठे व्यक्ति का जब दूसरे झूठे व्यक्ति से मेल होता है तो उसमें संसार के प्रति मोह दृढ़ होता है। किन्तु जब झूठे व्यक्ति को जगत की असत्यता और ब्रह्मा की सत्यता में निष्ठा वाला सन्त मिलता है, तभी संसार के प्रति उसकी आसक्ति नष्ट होती है।।83।।

जोरि करि जिबहै करै, है ज हलाल।

जब दफतर देखैगा दई, तब है,गा कौण हवाल।

काजी जीव को जबरदस्ती पकड़कर उसकी इच्छा के विरुद्ध हत्या करता है और उसे हलाल (धर्मानुकूल बलि) मानता है। लेकिन जब भगवान या विधाता उसके कर्मो का लेखा देखेगा, तब उस काजी की क्या दशा होगी।।84।।

तन कौ जोगी सब करैं, मन कौं बिरला कोइ।

सब सिंधि सहजै पाइए, जे मन जोगी होइ।

शरीर पर योगियों की सी वेष–भूषा तो हर कोई धारण कर लेता है। परन्तु सच्चे वैराग्य के द्वारा मन को कोई बिरला ही योगी बना पाता है। जिसका मन सच्चे योग को धारण कर लेता है, उसे सब प्रकार की सिद्धियाँ सहज ही प्राप्त हो जाती हैं।।85।।

तरवर तास बिलंबिए, बारह मास फलंत।

सीतल छाया गहर फल, पंषी केलि करंत।

उस वृक्ष का आश्रय लेना चाहिए जो बारहों महीनों हरा–भरा एवं फलवान रहता है। ऐसे वृक्ष की शीतल छाया रहती है और उसके खूब फल लगते हैं। उसमें पक्षी आनन्द से क्रीड़ा करते रहते हैं।।86।।

Jhoonte kon jhootha miley, doona badhe saneh|
Jhoonte koon sancha miley, tab hee toote neh||

When the two liars meet, their mortal bonds of affection get stronger. However, when a liar meets some one adhering to truth, his infatuation for this false world gets broken||83||

Joree kar jibhen karen, kahatey hain jie hahal|
Jab daphtar diekhedga dayee, tab hwega kon howal||

When a Quazi(Muslim) forcibly beheads a being he calls it a religious sacrifice. But when God's attendants scrutinise the Quazi's wordly deeds, what would be tbe verdict is quite understandable [i.e., won't the Quazi meet the same fate as that of the being which he forcibly sacrificed?]||84||

Tan kau jogi sab karen, man kon birlā koi|
Sab sindhi sahaje payeeye, je man jogi hoi||

Every one can pretend to be an eremite outwardly but the real one is that who by his beart has renounced the world. Such true hermits get automatically endowed with supernatural adeptness and all such powers||85||

Tarauvara tā s vilambiye, barah mas phalanta|
Seetal chhayā gahar phal, panshee keli karanta||

Seek shelter only beneath such a tree which is green and fruitful all the year round. Such trees have their shadows cool with lots of fruits sprouting in them. The birds also frolic only in such trees||86||

तूँ–तूँ करता तूँ भया, मुझ मैं रही न हूँ।
वारी फेरी बलि गई, जित देखौं तित तूँ।

'तू ही' 'तू ही' का'–अर्थात ब्रह्म के अतिरिक्त और किसी की सत्ता नहीं है – का मनन और ध्यान करते–करते रहते मुझ में अपना अहं–भाव ही नहीं रहा। जीवात्मा कह रही है कि मैं भगवान् पर न्यौछावर होती–होती उसको समर्पित ही हो गई हूँ। अब तो जिधर देखती हूँ, उधर केवल वही दिखाई देता है। जैसे प्रेमी को सारा जगत् प्रियतम दीखता है, वैसे ही जीव को सम्पूर्ण जगत् ही ब्रह्ममय दिखाई देने लगा है।।87।।

नर नारी सब नरक है, जब लग देह सकाम।
कहै कबीर ते राम के , जे सुमिरौं निहकाम ।

जब तक देह में वासना और इच्छा है तब तक सभी नर और नारी वास्तव में नरक रूप हैं। वासना के विषय स्वयं भी नरक रूप हैं। तथा परिणाम में भी केवल नरक के ही हेतु हो सकते हैं। जो निष्काम–भाव से भगवान् का स्मरण करता है, प्रेम के लिए ही प्रेम करता है, वही वस्तुतः भगवान् का प्रियजन है।।88।।

निंदक नेड़ा राखियै, आंगणि कुटी छवाहि।
बिन सावण पाणी बिन, निरमल करै सुभाइ।

अपने निंदक को अपने समीप हो, अपने आंगन में छप्पर डालकर रखना चाहिए। वह बिना साबुन और जल के व्यक्ति को सहज रूप में ही निर्मल कर देता है।।89।।

नैनं हमारे जलि गए, छिन छिन लोड़ै तुझ।
नां तँ मिलै न मैं खुसी, ऐसी बेदन मुझ।

है भगवान् हमारे नेत्र तुम्हारे विरह में जल गए हैं और क्षण–क्षण तुम्हें खोज रहे हैं। पर हे भगवान् न तुम मिले न मेरा हृदय उल्लसित हुआ। मुझे कितनी तीव्र वेदना है।?।।90।।

Toon-toon karatā toon bhaya, mujh men rahee na hoon|
Vā ri pheri bali gayee, jita dekhon tita toon||

Searching for the only True Entity and yelling for 'You-You' I have verily lost my own entity. I became so much engrossed in You(God) that I have lost all consciousness for other and see only God and only Him everywhere||87||

Nara-nā ri sab narak hai, jah lagi deha sakā m|
Kahe Kabir te Ram ke, je sumiren nihkā m||

Till the body has passions and lust, all men and women are the pockets of hell. It is only when one devotes one self dispassionately and with out any craving for any thing in return that one really becomes the beloved of Lord.||88||

Nindak nerhe rā khiye, angana kutee chhavā hi|
Bin sā bun pā nee bine, nirmal karei subhā hi||

One should ever keep one's columniator close to or soap the calumniator pups on wasting away one's vices or filth.||89||

Naina hamā re jali gaye, chhin-chhin laurhe tujjha|
Na toon mile na main khushee, eisee vedan mujjha||

O Lord! Searching ever for you my eyes have began to burn in the lust of separation from You. But neither could I meet you, nor my heart could exult in ecstasy. How fierce is my this agony of separation||90||

नैंनां अंतिर आव तूँ ज्यूँ हौं नैन झपेउँ।
नां हौं देखै और कुँ, नां तुझ देखन देउँ।

हे प्रिय, तुम मेरे नेत्रों में समा जाओ और मैं तुम्हारे वहाँ विराजने पर अपने नेत्रों को बंद कर लूँ, ताकि न तो मैं किसी अन्य को देखूँ और न तुम्हें किसी अन्य को देखने दूँ।।91।।

न्यंदक दूरि न कीजिए, दीजै आदर मान।
निरमल तन मन सब करै, बकि बकि आंनहि आंन।

अपने निंदक को दूर नहीं करना चाहिए। उसको आदर–सम्मान देना चाहिए। वह आत्मालोचन का भाव जगाकर मानव को शरीर और मन अर्थात अपने बाह्य और आभ्यन्तर सभी को निर्मल करने की प्रेरणा दे देता है।।92।।

परनारी परसुंदरी, बिरला बंचै कोइ।
खाताँ मीठी खाँड– सी , अंति कालि विष होइ।

दूसरे की स्त्री तथा दूसरे की प्रेमिका में अनुरक्त होने से कोई बिरला ही बचता है। वह खाने में अर्थात् भोग में खांड के समान मीठी अवश्य लगती है, परन्तु उसका परिणाम विष रूप ही है।।93।।

परनारी राता फिरै, चोरी बिढता खांहि।
दिवस चारि सरस रहै अंति समूला जाहि।

दूसरे की स्त्री से अनुराग करना चोरी की कमाई खाना है। इसमें व्यक्ति चार दिन के लिए भले ही फलता–फूलता रहे, परन्तु अन्त में वह समूल नष्ट हो जाता है।।94।।

पांहन कूँ का पूजिए जे जनम न देई जाव।
आंधा नर आसामुषी, यौही खोवै आव।

पत्थर की पूजा करने से क्या लाभ है? यह पत्थर जन्म–भर पूजने पर भी कभी किसी को कुछ कहता नहीं है। भक्त की प्रार्थना पर उत्तर नहीं दे पाता है। पर मानव आशाओं में फंसा हुआ अन्धा हो गया है और इसी से

Nainā antar ava toon, jyoon haun naina jhapeun|
Na haun dekhan aur koon, na tujha dekhan deun||

O, My Beloved! Enter into my eyes for ever and then I may close them finally. Then neither I may see anyone else nor may allow anyone else to see you||91||

Nindak doori na keejiye, deeje ā dar mā n|
Nirmal tan man sab kare, baki baki anahiā n||

One should not keep one's critic at a distance. On the contrary, such a person should be kept close in full comfort and honour because he rivets your attention to your flaws and short-comings and inspires you to get rid of them||92||

Paranā ri parsundari birlā bā nche koi|
Khatan meethi khanda-si, anti-kā li vish hoi||

Very rare are those that can successfully fight against the temptation of getting attracted to other's women or beautiful wenches. Initially they appear as sweet as a sugar candy on eating but ultimately they leave only toxic effect||93||

Paranā ri rata phiren, chori bidhata khā nhi|
Diwas chari sarasa rahi, anta samoolā jā nhi||

Loving other's women is tentamount to enjoying on the stolen wealth. For a few days one might prosper but ultimately one gets destroyed totally||94||

Pā han koon kā poojiye, je janam na deyi jā b|
Andha nara asā mukhee, yonhee khoye ā b||

Worshipping stone idols is just meaningless. No matter you worship them for your entire life they won't(or can't) respond to you prayers. Yet blinded by his mad desire man

व्यर्थ ही मूर्ति–पूजा में अपनी प्रतिष्ठा और शक्ति गँवा रहा है।।95।।

पांहण केरा पूतला, करि पूजै करतार।
इही भरोसै जे रहे, ते बूडे काली धार।

जो पत्थर की मूर्ति को ही सृष्टिकर्त्ता मानकर पूजता है, और इसी मूर्तिपूजा के बल पर अपने उद्धार की आशा करता है, वह संसार–समुद्र की गहरी भयानक धार में डूब जाता है।।96।।

पारब्रह्म के तेज का, कैसा है उनमान।
कहिबे कूँ सोभा नहीं, देख्या ही परवान।

पारब्रह्म के प्रकाश का क्या अनुमान लगाया जा सकता है? उसका सौन्दर्य वाणी का विषय नहीं। वह साक्षात् अनुभूति का ही विषय है।।97।।

पूत पियारो पिता कौं, गौहनि लागो धाइ।
लाभ मिठाई हाथि दे, आपण गयो भुलाइ।

पिता का प्रिय पुत्र दौड़कर उसके साथ हो लिया। पिता ने लोभ–रूपी मिठाई उसके हाथ में दे दी। यह बालक उसी में रमकर अपने आपको भूल गया और उससे पिता का साथ छूट गया।।98।।

पोथी पढ़ि पढ़ि जग मुवा, पंडित भया न कोइ।
ऐकै आषिर पीव का, पढ़ैं सु पंडित होइ।

यह सारा संसार इन पुस्तकों को पढ़ते–पढ़ते मर गया है, पर इनमें से कोई वास्तविक पंडित नहीं हुआ। जो अपने पति–परमेश्वर के नाम का एक अक्षर भी पढ़ लेता है, वही उत्कृष्ट पंडित बन जाता है।।99।।

प्रेम गली अति साँकरी तामे दो न समाय।
जब मैं था तब हरि नहीं, जब हरि हैं मैं नाहिं।

प्रेम की गली अत्यधिक सँकरी है। वहाँ दो नहीं समा सकते (द्वैत भाव का प्रवेश वहाँ हो ही नहीं सकता)। जब तक मुझमें अहंकार विद्यमान था, तब तक ईश्वर वहाँ नहीं था और जब से ईश्वर का प्रवेश हुआ है, मेरा अहंकार

keeps on worshipping them still.||95||

Pā han kera pootala, kari puje kartā r|
Ihee bharose je rā he, te boode kā li dhar||

He who worships the stone-idols as though they are gods and hopes for his redemption ultimately gets drowned in this mundane ocean's most deadly waves||96||

Parbhramma ke tej kā, kaisa hai unmā n|
Kahibe koon sobhā nahin, dekhyā hee parvan||

Can the divine light's illumination be ever estimated? Its beatific vision transcends description since that can only be realised inwardly||97||

Poota piyaro pita kau, gauhani lago dhai|
Lobha mithā yee hā thi dey, apanā gayo bhulai||

A beloved son of a father dashed to se ek his father's company. When the father offered him tempting sweets, the son got engrossed in the sweet and forgot about his father.[In this mataphor the son is man, the father God and the sweets wordly temptation]||98||

Pothi padhi-padhi jug muaa, pundit bhayā na koya|
Ekei akhar peeva kā, padhe so pundit hoya||

No matter the whole world exhausts itself to death by reading huge tomes and books no one from it can become the wise or learned in the real sense. Only if one masters just one letter signifying the Supreme Beloved(God), one becomes the real pundit||99||

Prem-gali ati sā nkari, tā me do no samahin|
Jab men thā tab Hari nahin, jab Hari hain men nā hin||

The lane of love is too narrow to accommodate two

समाप्त हो गया है।।100।।

प्रेम ढूँढ़त मैं फिरौं, प्रेमी मिलै न कोइ।
प्रेमी कौं प्रेमी मिलैं सब विष अमृत होइ।

कबीर कहते हैं कि मैं भगवान के प्रेमी को ढूँढता फिरता हूँ। पर मुझे कोई सच्चा प्रेमी भी नहीं मिला। जब भगवान के प्रेमी से प्रेमी मिलता है, तब यह विषय–वासनाओं का सारा विष, अमृत में परिणित हो जाता है। क्योंकि उस समय ईश्वर–प्रेम का प्रवाह फूट पड़ता है।।101।।

प्रेम न खेतौं नीपजै, प्रेम न हाटि बिकाइ।
राजा परजा जिस रुचे, सीस देइ लै जाइ।

प्रेम अत्यन्त ही दुर्लभ वस्तु है। यह खेतों में पैदा नहीं होता है, कि इसका बाहुल्य हो। यह सामान्यतः बाजार में बिकने वाली वस्तु नहीं है, कि चाहे जो इसे खरीद ले। यह अमूल्य एवं दुष्प्राप्य वस्तु है। राजा–प्रजा में जिस किसी को इसकी चाह होती है उसे अपना सिर देकर(अपना अहं समर्पित करके) इसे लेना पड़ता है।।102।।

निस अँधियारी कारणैं, चौरासी लख चंद।
अति आतुर ऊदै किया, तऊ दिष्टि नहिं मंद।

अज्ञान की अंधेरी रात को प्रकाशित करने के लिए अनन्त आतुरता से जीव ने चौरासी लाख योनि रुप चन्द्रमा उदित कर लिए हैं परन्तु इस मंद बुद्धि को दृष्टि प्राप्त नहीं हुई अर्थात ज्ञान प्राप्त नहीं हुआ।।103।।

पांणी ही तैं पातला, धूँवाँ हीं त क्षीण।
पवनाँ बेगि उतावला, दोसत कबीरैं कीन्ह।

कबीर कहते हैं कि हमने ऐसा मित्र बनाया है जो जल से भी पतला है, धूम्र से अधिक क्षीण है और जिसमें पवन से अधिक वेग है।।104।।

beings. Consequently when I am here Hari is not, when Hari is there I am absent[Meaning love needs total coalescence of two identities with no trace of duality].||100||

Premi dhoondhat men phiron, premi mile na koi|
Premi eon premi milen, sab vish amnita hoi||

Kabir says I ever go on searching for the true lover[of God] but I fail to meet one. Only when a beloved gets a beloved that all that is toxic becomes nectareous||101||

Prem na kheti neepaje, prem na hati bikaya|
Raja parja jo ruche, seesh deyi le jaiya||

Love is neither produced in the fields nor it is available in the market. Whoever wants it whether the king or the ryot-procure it aginst the sacrifice of the head[i.e., love is available for those who can eliminate their ego-sense]||102||

Nisa andhiyāri karanen, chaurāsi lakh chandā|
Ati atur oodey kiya, tauoo dishti nahin manda||

In order to illunine the dark might of ignorance the infinite impatience of the beings have created 8.4 million moons yet the dismal-sighted failed to see the real light of knowledge[Traditional belief is that there are 8.4 million species in this world] .||103||

Pāni heen ten pātalā, dhoovan hee ten ksheena|
Pavana begi utāvalā, dosat Kabiren keena||

Kabir says that I have developed friendship with some one who is subtler than water and fainter that smoke but who is mightier than even the wind||104||

बिरह जलाई मैं जलौं, जलती जलहरि जाऊँ।
मो देख्यौ जलहरि जलै, संतौ कहाँ बुझाऊँ।

जीवात्मा कह रही है कि मैं विरह से जलाई हुई जल रही हूँ और इसी अवस्था में जल के स्थान पर अपनी आग बुझाने के लिए जाता हूँ तो वह जल का आगार भी मेरी आग से जलने लगता है। हे सन्तो, कहो अब यह आग कहाँ बुझाऊँ? ।।105।।

बिरह भुजंगम तन बसै, मंत्र न लागै कोई।
राम वियोगी ना जिवै, जिवै तो बौरा होइ।

विरह–रूपी सर्प हृदय में ही निवास करता है। वह निरन्तर डसता रहता है। अब इस तन पर मंत्रादिक के उपचार नहीं चल सकते हैं। राम से वियुक्त जीव जी नहीं सकता है। अगर जीता है तो पागल ही रहता है। अर्थात् सांसारिक विषयों के ग्रहण की दृष्टि से पागल–सा हो जाता है।।106।।

बैद मुवा रोगी मुवा, मुवा सकल संसार।
एक कबीरा ना मुवा, जिनि के राम अधार।

वैद्य भी मर गया और रोगी भी मर गया। सारा संसार ही मर गया कबीर कहते हैं, कि केवल कबीर अथवा वह व्यक्ति अर्थात् भक्त जिसने भगवान की शरण ली है, वह नहीं मरा।।107।।

मरते–मरते जग मुआ, औरस मुआ न कोय।
दास कबीरा यों मुआ, बहुरि न मरना होय।

कबीर कहते हैं कि मरते–मरते तो जग मरता रहता है, फिर भी कोई सम्यक् रूप से नहीं मरता। लेकिन कबीर तो ऐसा मरा कि फिर (दुबारा) मरना ही नहीं हुआ। अभिप्राय यह है कि इस तरह जीना कि फिर जन्म न हो। इस प्रकार मरना कि फिर मृत्यु न हो। जन्म होगा तो मृत्यु होगी ही। जब पुनः जन्म ही न होगा तो पुनः मृत्यु भी न होगी।।108।।

Biraha jalayee main jalon, jalati jalahar jauon|
Mo dekhyo jalahari jalei, Santo kahan buhjuon||

The soul says that I am burning in the fire of seperation from my eloved. But when I go to a water source to douse my fire, owing to the heat of my fire even the water source starts burning as well. Tell me O holymen(saints) where should I go to douse it ||105||

Biraha bhujangam tan base, mantra na lāge koi|
Ram viyogi na jive, jive to baura hoi||

The serpent of the grief of seperation dwells in the heart of the lover which keeps on biting. No treatment to cure this agony ever succeeds. In fact the soul seperated from Supreme soul(Ram) just can't survive. Even if it lives it becomes mad(owing to the worldly atturements.)||106||

Baid muva rogi muva, muva sakal sansār|
Ek Kabira na muva, jin ke Rām adhār||

The physician and the patient both are dead. In fact the whole world is dead[so it appears]. Only Kabir[or that devotee] manages to survive in reality whose faith is based on Ram||107||

Marte marte jag muaa, auras muaa na koya|
Das Kabeera yon muaa, bahuri na marna hoya||

Kabir says that though this whole world[i.e., every being] always keeps on dying, no one dies finally[i.e., the soul comes back in different form]. But Kabir alone dies in such a way as to never come back in this world[i.e., his soul attains salvation or Moksha]||108||

माया की झल जग जल्या, कनक कांमणीं लागि।
कहु धौं किहि विधि राखियै, रूई लपेटी आगि।

कंचन और कामिनी के मोह में यह सारा संसार माया की अर्थात् विषय–भोगों की ज्वाला में जल गया है। कहो तो रूई में लिपटी आग को प्रज्वलित होने एवं उसे रूई को भस्म करने से कैसे रोका जा सकता है।।109।।

भारी कहौं तो बहु डरूँ, हलका कहूँ तो झूठ।
मैं का जानूँ राम कूँ, नैनँ कबहूँ न दीठ।

कबीर कहते हैं कि परमात्मा को हलका कहूँ तो झूठ कह रहा हूँ, क्योंकि वह हलका नहीं है। वह भारी है। लेकिन भारी कहने से भी डर लगता है, क्योंकि वह छिद्र में भी छिपा हुआ है। वास्तविकता तो यह है कि मैं राम के विषय में कुछ भी नहीं जानता क्योंकि मैंनें अपनी आँखों से उसे कभी देखा ही नहीं है।।110।।

भूखा भूखा क्या करैं, कहा सुनावै लोग।
भांडा घड़ि जिनि मुख दिया, सोई पूरण जोग।

रे जीव ! 'भूखा हूँ'–'भूखा हूँ' की रट क्यों लगा रखी है? लोंगों को क्यों सुना रहा है? जिसने इस शरीर रूपी घड़े को बनाया है, जिसने इसे मुख दिया है, वही घट और मुख को भरेगा भी।।111।।

मन कै मतै न चालिए, छांड़ि जीव की वांणि।
ताकू केरे सूत ज्यूँ उलटि अपूठा आंणि।

कबीरदास कहते हैं कि हे साधक! तुझे मन के पीछे नहीं चलना चाहिए(मन की उमंगों के अनुसार आचरण नहीं करना चाहिए।) तू अपनी इस आदत को छोड़ दे। तू अपने आपको संसार से विरक्त करके ब्रह्म में उसी प्रकार लगा दे जिस प्रकार तकुए द्वारा काता गया कच्चा सूत फिर उसी में लपेट दिया जाता है।।112।।

Māyā ki jhal jag jalya, kanak kāmini lagi|
Kahudhon kihi vidhi rākhiye, ruyee lapetee āgi||

The whole world burns in the temptation wrought by maya through the charms of comely women and gold. But how can the piece of cotton enshrining fire can be saved from incineration||109||

Bhari kahoon to bahu danroon, halka kahuoon to jhootha|
Main ka janoon Ram koon, nainoon kabahoon na deetha||

Kabir says that if I call Supreme Lord to be light it is a blatant lie because He is not so. However if I say He is heavy, I am afraid that is also not true either because He permeates even in the smallest space. In fact I know nothing about Ra¯ m(Him) because I have never seen Him with my eyes||110||

Bhookha-bhookha kya kāre, kahā sunave log|
Bhandā gharhi jini mukh diya soyee pooran jog||

O Man! Why do you keep yelliing : 'I'm hungry-I'm hungry' and tell people about it.[No one will provide you food]. He who has given you a mouth shall also give you food; He who makes the pitcher also provides contents to fill it and sustain it ||111||

Man kei matei na chāliye, chharhi jeeva ki vāni|
Takoo kere soota jyoon, ulati apootha āni||

Kabir says that O aspirant! Never follow the dictates of your whims[control your mind]. Shed your this habit. Become averse to this false world and devote your total concentration to Lord Supreme the same way as the thread spun by the bobbin gets wrapped round the bobbin itself||112||

मन जाणैं सब बात, जाणत ही औगुण करै।
काहे की कुसलात, कर दीपक कूँ वै पड़ै।

मन जानता सब–कुछ है, पर वह जान बूझकर ही अनुचित काम करता रहता है। (विषय–वासनाओं के बंधन करने वाले स्वरूप से परिचित होते हुए भी मन का स्वभाव ही उनमें लिप्त हो जाने का है।) कुशल–क्षेम कैसे रह सकती है जब दीपक हाथ में लेकर (मार्ग देखता हुआ भी स्वेच्छा से ही जानते हुए ही) भी मनुष्य कुएँ में गिर पड़ता है।।1 1 3।।

माया तजी तौ का भया, मानि तजी नहीं जाइ।
मानि बड़े मुनियर गिले, मानि सबनि कौं खाइ।

कबीर कहते हैं कि धन छोड़ दिया तो क्या हुआ? सम्मान की आकांक्षा तथा उससे प्रभावित होने की दुर्बलता तो छूटी नहीं। सम्मान और उसकी आकांक्षा से बड़े–बड़े मुनि भी नष्ट हो गए हैं। सम्मान की आकांक्षा से सम्पूर्ण जगत् ग्रसित है।।1 1 4।।

माया दीपक नर पतंग, भ्रमि–भ्रमि इवै पड़ंत।
कहै कबीर गुर ग्यान थै (तै) एक आध उबरंत।

माया रूपी दीपक के लिए नर पतंग रूप है। मानव घूम–घूम कर अर्थात् अनेक योनियों में भटकता हुआ तथा अज्ञान में भूला हुआ इसी आग में ऐसे ही जलता है। बस, गुरू के ज्ञान से कोई एकाध ही इस आग से बच पाता है।।1 1 5।।

माया मुई न मन मुआ, मरि मरि गया सरीर।
आसा त्रिष्णाँ नाँ मुई, यौं कहि गया दासकबीर।

न माया (वासना) मरती है न मन ही। शरीर शक्तिहीन होकर मृतवत् हो जाता है परन्तु आशा और तृष्णा बनी ही रहती है। उन्हीं वासनाओं के वशीभूत होकर शरीर जन्म–मरण में चक्कर काटता रहता है।।1 1 6।।

Man jane sab bāt, janata hee augun kare|
Kāhe ki kushalāt, kar deepak koove pare||

Despite the human mind being aware what is good and what is not it gets drawn to committing improper actions. How can there be welfare of the one who falls into the well on his way when he holds a lamp in his hand? [Meaning thereby that man gets allured by sensual temptations even when he knows them to be no good. It is not due to ignorance as it is his deliberate distraction].

Māyā tajee tau ka bhayā, māni tajee nahin jai|
Mani bare muniyar gale, mani sabani kau khai||

Kabir says that leaving temptations for worldly pleasures is not enough.[Unless one sheds one's ego and arrogance one may not came on to the righteous way]. But shedding ego is very difficult a many high sages have suffered doom due to their arrogance. Ego afflicts the whole world||113||

Mā yā deepak nara patang, bhrami-bhrami evei paranta|
Kahe Kabir Guru gyan thei, eka adha ubaranta||

If ma¯ ya¯ (wordly temptations and illusions) is a lighted lamp, man is a fire-fly who through various species keeps on striking at the flame in a confused state. Only rarely some escape getting burnt in this fire owing to the enlightenment received from the Guru||115||

Maya muyee na man muaa, mari mari gaya sareera|
Āshā trishna na muyee, yon kahi gaya dās Kabir||

Neither ma¯ ya¯ (passion) dies nor mind's attachment to it. The body becomes powerless and utimately perishes but neither hope nor longing ever leaves it. Says Kabir that

माला पहरया कुछ नहीं, काती मन के साथि।
जब लग हरि प्रगटै नहीं, तब लग पड़ता हाथि।

अगर मन रागद्वेष की कैंची चलाता रहे तो साधु वेश धारण करने के लिए माला पहनना व्यर्थ है। जब तक भगवान् अन्तःकरण में प्रकट नहीं होते (अर्थात् सच्ची भक्ति तथा जीवन की पवित्रता नहीं जागती) तब तक मनुष्य पर माया के हाथ पड़ते रहते हैं।।116।।

माला पहरैं मनमुषी, ताथैं कछू न होइ।
मन माला कौं फेरताँ, जग उजियारा सोइ।

व्यक्ति मन की वासनाओं की ओर उन्मुख रहकर माला पहनता है, उससे कुछ भी लाभ नहीं है। मन रूपी माला को फेरने से ही व्यक्ति को परमतत्व का प्रकाश मिलता है।।117।।

माला पहरयाँ कुछ नहीं, भगति न आई हाथि।
माथौ मूछँ मुँडाइ करि, चल्या जगत कै साथि।

अगर भक्ति–भावना नहीं जागी तो माला पहनना व्यर्थ ही रहा। व्यक्ति सिर और मूँछों का मुण्डन कराकर अर्थात् संन्यासी का वेश धारण करके भी भक्ति के अभाव में जगत् के साथ चलता रहता है। (अर्थात् वह भी विषयी संसार की तरह लोक–व्यवहार करता है।) ।।118।।

माषी गुड़ मैं गाड़ि रही, पंष रही लपटाइ।
ताली पीटै सिरि धुनैं, मींठे बोई माइ।

मक्खी गुड़ में धँस गई है और उसके पंख उसके चेप से लिपट गए हैं। वह सिर धुनती है और हाथ मलती है, अब उसमें उड़ने की शक्ति नहीं रह गई है। रे सखी, मीठे ने उसे नष्ट कर दिया है।।119।।

this way body continues to suffer these death and life cycles travails||115||

Mālā paharyā kuchha nahin, kāti man ke saathi|
Jab lagi Hari pragtai nahin, tab lagi parhatā hāthi||

Wearing holy beads and donning ochre robes is meaningless till one's heart is full of affection and ill-will. So man keeps on falling prey to mā yā 's temptations till real God-realisation dawns in one's heart||116||

Mala paharen manamushi, tatten kachhu na hoi|
Man mala kon pheratā, jag ujiyara soi||

If passions and worldly temptations keep on assailing one's heart there is little sense in pretending to be an ascetic wearing string of holy beads. It is only when the mind's bead is repeatedly inspected and observed that the real enlightenment dawns in one" heart||117||

Mala paharyan kuch nahin, bhagati na ayee hāth|
Matho mooncha mudaikar, chalya jagat ke sāth||

If the real sense of devotion doesn't engender in one's heart what is the purpose of wearing the string of beads, shaving off one's head and face hair and donning the ochre robes? The lack of real urge for devotion would only make one follow the world blindly and succumb to worldly temptation||118||

Manshi gur men garhi rahi, pankha rahi lapitayi|
Tali peete siri dhune, meeta boyee mayi||

Temptation landed a fly in jaggery and the viscous sweetness trapped its wings also. Now no matter how

मूरष संग न कीजिए, लोहा जलि न तिराइ।
कदली–सीप–भुवंग–मुषि, एक बूँद तिहुँ भाइ।

मूर्ख का संसर्ग नहीं रखना चाहिए। लोहा जल में नहीं तैर सकता है। (अर्थात् जैसे लोहे का आश्रय लेकर समुद्र पार करने की भावना वाला व्यक्ति डूबता ही है, वैसे ही मूर्ख के आश्रय से भी जीव संसार–समूह में डूबता ही है।) एक ही बूँद के कदली सीप और सर्प के मुख में जाने से तीन भिन्न परिणाम होते हैं। (वह क्रमशः कपूर, मोती और विष में परिणत हो जाती है।)।।120।।

मेरै मन मैं पड़ि गई, ऐसी एक दरार।
फाटा फटक पषाण ज्यूँ, मिल्या न दूजी बार।

कबीर कहते हैं कि मेरे मन में संसार से वैराग्य की एक ऐसी दरार पड़ गई है कि वह स्फटिक पाषाण–खण्ड की तरह अन्त में फटकर जगत् से पूर्णतया अलग ही हो गया। उसके बाद वह फिर से सांसारिक विषयों में रमा ही नहीं।)।।121।।

मैं जांण्यूँ पढ़िबौ भलौ, पढ़िबा थै भलि जोग।
राँम नाँम सूँ प्रीति करि, भल भल नींदौ लोग।

मैं समझता था कि पुस्तकों का पढ़ना अच्छा है। परन्तु इस शुष्क शब्द–ज्ञान की अपेक्षा उस परम तत्त्व से योग प्राप्त करने की साधना कही अधिक अच्छी है। अतः हे जीव! राम के नाम से प्रेम कर, चाहे संसार इसके लिए तेरी निंदा ही करे।।122।।

माला पहरयाँ कुछ नहीं, गाँठि हिरदा की खोइ।
हरि चरनूँ चित राखिये, तौ अमरापुर होइ।

माला पहनने से कुछ भी लाभ नहीं है। अपने हृदय की कुटिलता तथा

valiantly it tries it is not capable of flying away anymore. Oh dear! The sweet temptation has killed the fly.[So is the situation of human-being with regard to sensual pleasures of the world].||119||

Moorakh sang na keejiye, loha jal na tirāya|
Kadali-seep-bhuvang-mushee, ek boond tihu bhāya||

Like an iron rod can't help one swim across a water course since iron gets easily drowned in water, so also is the company of fools in this mundane ocean[It will also cause your doom]. Hence never be associated with fools. On the other hand, if you have conducive company even a little of it yields good result. Just a drop of water in accordance with the company yields camphor for banana plants, pearl for an oyster shell and poison for a snake||120||

Mere man main pari gayee, eisee ek darār|
Phata phatak pashan jyoon, milya na dooji bār||

Says Kabir that aversion to mundane affairs has created such a split in my mind that I never sought to be associated with them. It is like a split in a marble slab; the final line of division between its two pieces.||121||

Main janyoon padhibo bhalo, padhya the bhali jog|
Ram nam soon preeti kari, bhali-bhali needan log||

Although reading books is good yet much bitter than accummulating this dry and bookish knowledge is seeking communion with the ultimate for enlightenment. So, O soul! be devoted to Ram even if the world censures you for being indifferent to it||122||

Mala paharyan kuchh nahin, gantha hridaya ki khoi|

संदेहों की गाँठ दूर करो। अगर भगवान् के चरणों में चित्त को लगा दोगे तो संसार ही स्वर्ग बन जाएगा।।123।।

यहु ऐसा संसार है, जैसा सैंबल फूल।
दिन दस के व्यौहार कौं, झूठे रंगि न भूलि।

यह संसार सेमर के फूल की तरह तत्त्वहीन, क्षण–स्थायी एंव भ्रम में डालने वाला है। यह जगत् दस दिन का व्यवहार है। इस संसार के क्षणिक एवं झूठे आकर्षण में जीव को अपना वास्तविक स्वरूप नहीं भूलना चाहिए।।124।।

यहु तन काचा कुंभ है, चोट चहूँ दिसि खाइ।
एक राम के नाँव बिन, जदि तदि परलै जाइ।

यह शरीर कच्चा घड़ा है। इस पर चारों ओर से माया, मोह और कर्म की चोट लग रही है। राम–नाम के अभाव में यह शरीर चाहे जब नष्ट हो जाएगा।।125।।

यहु तन जालौं मसि करूँ, ज्यूँ धूवाँ जाइ सरग्गि।
मति वै राम दया करै, बरसि बुझावै अग्गि।

मैं इस शरीर को जलाकर इस प्रकार भस्म कर दूँ कि इसके जलने का धुआँ स्वर्ग तक पहुँच जाए। संभव है कि भगवान् दया करके स्नेह की वर्षा से मेरी विरहाग्नि को बुझा दें।।126।।

यहु तन जालौं मसि करों, लिखों राम का नाउँ।
लेखणि करौं करंक की, लिखि–लिखि राम पठाउँ।

मैं इस शरीर को जलाकर स्याही बना लूँगी और अपने इस नर–कंकाल की लेखनी तैयार करूँगी। बस इसी से लिख–लिख कर राम को प्रेम–संदेश भेजती रहूँगी।।127।।

Hari charanoon chita rakhiye, tan amarā pur hoi||

No use wearing the string of the holy beads. It is better you remove the complexes and confusions possessing your heart, man! If you can devote your concentration to the feet of God, perhaps you well see the heaven on this earth for yourself||123||

Yahu eisa sansār hai, jaisa saimal phool|
Din dasa ke vyavahar kon, jhoothi rangi na bhooli||

This world is juice-less, transistory and confusing like the cotton plant.[confusing because its flowers are no flowers in reality]. While stay here is only for a few days, one should not overlook the reality of one's essential entity and stay clear of the worldly temptations as they too, are fey||124||

Yeh tan kānchā kumbha hai, chot chahun this khāi|
Ek Rām ke nam bin, jadi tadi paraley jai||

This body is like a raw earthen pitcher ever receiving blows from a variety of temptations, and duty-bound actions. It is only the name of Ram that is sustaining it, else it would have been destroyed in no time.||125||

Yahu tan jalon masi karoon, jyon dhooan jai saraggi|
Mati vei Ram daya kare, barasi bujhave aggi||

I want to burn my body in such a way as to make the smoke from it reach the heavens. May be, then Ram sheds His grace on my soul and rain love to douse the fire of my agony due to seperation from Him.||126||

Tahu tan jalon masi karon, likhon Ram kan naun|
Lekhan karon karanka ki, likhi-likhi Ram pathaun||

[The soul says]: "I would burn my body and create

राता माता नाम का, पीया प्रेम अघाय।
मतवाला दीदार का, माँगे मुक्ति बलाय।

कबीर कहते हैं कि जो उस परमात्मा के प्रेम–रस में मस्त हो गया, जिसने प्रेम–रस को छक कर पी लिया, वह परमात्मा के दर्शन से मस्त हुआ प्राणी मोक्ष की कामना ही नहीं करता। बला से उसे मुक्ति मिले या न मिले।।128।।

राम नाम जाण्यां नहीं, पाल्यो कटक कुटंब।
धंधा ही में मरि गया, बाहर हुई न बंब।

हे मानव, राम के नाम को तो तूने जानो ही नहीं। तू अपने कुटुम्ब की सेना को ही पालता रहा। धंधा करता हुआ(अर्थात् निजी स्वार्थ के सांसारिक कार्य करता हुआ) ही मर गया। इससे परलोक में तेरा यशोगान नहीं हो सका।।129।।

हेरत–हेरत हे सखो, रह्या कबीर हिराइ।
बूँद समाणी समद में, सो कत हेरी जाइ।

हे सखि, अपने आत्म–स्वरूप को खोजते–खोजते कबीर स्वयं खो गया है। (उसका अहं व्यापक चैतन्य में विलीन हो गया है।) जो बूँद समुद्र में मिल गई है, जिसका अब पृथक् आस्तित्व नहीं रह गया है, वह भला कैसे ढूँढ़ी जा सकती है? (जीव का पृथक् अहं जब परमात्म–चैतन्य में विलीन हो जाता है तब उसकी पृथकता का भान कैसे सम्भव है?)।।130।।

हम देखत जग जात है, जग देखत हम-जांह।
ऐसा कोई नां मिलै, पकड़ि छुड़ावैं बांह।

हमारे देखते हुए संसार काल के मुख में जा रहा है और संसार के देखते

ink from its ashes. I would convert my skeleton into a pen to keep on writing and sending my love messages to Ram[the Supreme soul].||127||

Rata mata nam kak, peeya prem aghā ya|
Matwā lā didā r kā, mange mukti balā ya||

Kabir says that he who has imbibed the juice of divine love to his hearts-fill becomes so ecstatically intoxicated that he even doesn't crave for Salvation and Moksha. Then he cares two boots for all kinds of final release of the soul.||128||

Rā m nā m jā nyan nahin, pā lyo katak kutumba|
Dhandha hee main mari gaya, bā har hui na bamba||

O Man! You could not learn the real value of chanting Ram's name. You just fulfilled your worldly duties and died, leaving nothing to the other world. With the result in the other world your paens couldn't echo||129||

Herat-herat he sakho, rahya Kabir hiraye|
Boond samani samad men, so kat heri jaye||

O dear! Kabir has been lost to his own self in his search of the self in him. How a drop mingling in the ocean can again be identified and located[Perfect coalescence preludes identification of the previous form]||130||

Hum dekhat jag jā t hain, jag dekhat hum janhi|
Eisa koi na milei, pakadhi chhudave bā nha||

I behold the world sliding down the jaws of time and the world sees me getting into that also. I couldn't get such a guru who could have held me back to release me from

हुए हम वहाँ से चले जाएँगे। ऐसा कोई गुरू नहीं मिला जो काल से बाँह छुड़ाकर हमें मुक्त कर लेता।।131।।

हम भी पांहन पूजते, ढोते रन के रोझ।
सतगुरू की किरपा भई, डारया सिर थे बोझ।

कबीर कहते हैं कि हम पर सतगुरू की कृपा हो गई है। इससे हमने अन्धविश्वासों के बोझ को अपने सिर से पटक दिया है अन्यथा हम भी उनमें फँसे हुए पत्थर की पूजा करते और जलहीन सूखे जंगल की नीलगाय की तरह उभय–भ्रष्ट एवं अनुपयोगी होकर भटकते–फिरते।।132।।

हिरदा भीतरि दौं बलै, धुंवा न परगट होइ।
जाकै लागी सो लखै, कै जिहि लाई सोइ।

विरही के हृदय में अग्नि जलती है, परंतु उसका धुआँ तक बाहर प्रकट नहीं होता है। उस अग्नि का ज्ञान या तो उसे होता है जिसके हृदय में यह लगी है या उसे जिसने यह आग लगाई है।।133।।

विषै कर्म की केंचुली, पहरि हुआ नर नाग।
सिर फोड़ै सूझै नहीं, कोउ आगिला अभाग।

विषय–वासना की केंचुली पहिन कर मनुष्य सर्प के समान बन गया है। अनेक प्रकार से प्रयास करता है और जीवन का मार्ग ढूँढ़ने के लिए प्रयत्न करता है परंतु वासना में अन्धा होने के कारण उसे मार्ग सूझता नहीं,(अर्थात् इसे ईश्वर–प्रेम का रास्ता नहीं दिखाई देता है।) यह इस जीव के पूर्व जन्म के पापों का ही परिणाम है।।134।।

संत न छाड़ै संतई, जे कोटिक मिलैं असंत।
चंदन भुवंगा बैढ़िया, तउ सीतलता न तजंत।

संत अपने साधु–स्वभाव को नहीं छोड़ता है चाहे उसे कितने ही असंतों का

this process||131||

Hum bhee pāhan poojatey, dhote ran ke rojh|
Sat guru ki kirpa bhayee, darya sir the bojh||

I could afford to throw down the heavy load of superstition only because I was fortunate to receive the Guru's grace. Else, I would have also been carrying the dead load of stone worship and would have roamed about listlessly in the dry and waterless jungles like 'neelgaya'[a worthless being].||132||

Hirada bheetari daun bale, dhuvan nā pargat hoi|
Jaken lagi so lakhe, kai jihi layee soi||

The fire of seperation rages inside the heart but its smoke is not seen anywhere. It is felt only by two : one who causes it and one who bears it||133||

Vishe karm ki kenchuli, pahani hua nar nāg|
Sir phode sòojhe nahin, kouoo āgila abhag||

Donning the slough of sensual attraction and their gratifications man has become almost a snake himself. Owing to getting blinded by passions and lusts he fails to find the right course of life[i.e., fails to seek the path towards God-realisation]. This is nothing but the consequence of his misdeeds in the past lives||134||

Sant na chhāde santayi je kotik milentasant|
Chandan bhujanga bathiya, tau seealta na tajant||

The noble never shed their nobel conduct no matter

मुकाबला करना पड़े। चंदन से अनेक सर्प लिपटे रहते हैं पर फिर भी वह अपनी शीतलता का परित्याग नहीं करता है।।1 3 5।।

सतगुरू साँचा, सूरिवाँ, तातैं लोहि लुहार।
कसणी दे कंचन किया, ताइ लिया ततसार।

सद्गुरू सच्चा वीर है। जैसे गर्म लोहे के लिए लुहार है, वैसे ही वैराग्य की अग्नि में तपे हुए शिष्य के लिए गुरू है। कसाव का पुट लगाकर एवं तप्त लोहे की तरह अग्नि में डाल–डालकर तथा पीट–पीट कर गुरू भी शिष्य को कंचन बना देता है, अर्थात् उसे ज्ञान की अग्नि में तपाकर उसके वास्तविक स्वरूप को, माया के विजातीय तत्त्व से पृथक् कर देता है।।1 3 6।।

सहज–सहज सब कोउ कहै, सहज न चीन्हैं कोइ।
जिन्ह सहजै विषिया तजी, सहज कहीजै सोई।

'सहज' 'सहज' कहकर उसकी बात तो सब करते हैं, पर वास्तव में उस सहज के स्वरूप को कोई पहचानता नहीं है। जो व्यक्ति सहज रूप में ही, स्वभावतः ही विषयों की आसक्ति छोड़ देता है, वही वास्तव में 'सहज' अवस्था को प्राप्त होता है।।1 3 7।।

सांई सूँ सब होत है, बंदै थै कुछ नांहि।
राई थै परबत करै, परबत राई मांहि।

भगवान् सर्वशक्तिमान है। उसके करने से ही सब कुछ होता है, मनुष्य के करने से कुछ भी नहीं। भगवान् सब असम्भवों को सम्भव कर देते हैं। राई से पर्वत कर देते हैं और पर्वत को राई में विलीन कर देते हैं।।1 3 8।।

सतगुर ऐसा चाहिए, ज्यों सिकलीगर होइ।
सबद मसकला फेरि कें, देह द्रपन करै सोई।

गुरू को सिकलीगर के समान होना चाहिए जो तत्त्व–ज्ञान के शब्दों के मसकले (शान रखने का चक्र) पर रगड़कर मुमुक्षु शिष्य के अन्तःकरण को

they come across scores of the vile persons. The sandalwood tree doesn't shed its coolness not withstanding many poisonous snakes ever wrapping it||135||

Satguru sancha sooriman, taten loha luhār|
Kasani dey kanchan kiya, tai liya tatasar||

Satguru[the true guru] is as valiant as the iron smith that moulds the molten iron into the desired form by beating it from all sides and shaping it to the desired pattern. In fact the real guru makes his disciple as good as gold by melting away the latter's flaws by his fire of knowledge.||136||

Sahaj-sahaj sab koi kahe, sahaj na cheehe koi|
Jin sahaje vishya taji, sahaj kaheeje soi||

All claim that it is easy to get rid of the sensual temptations but no one does so because, in fact, they don't know that state. Those who do leave such temptations effortlessly and they deserve to be called the real ascetics||137||

Sai soon sab hota hai, bande the kachhu nāhi|
Rai the parvat kare, parvat rai mā nhi||

God is omnipotent and everthing happens by His instigation. Man is really powerless. It is only God that can create a mountain out of a mole-bill and a mole-bill out of a mountain||138||

Satguru eisa chahiye, jyon sikligar hoi|
Sabad maskala pher ken, deha drapan kare soi||

The real guru ought to be like a whettor to sharpen his disciple's intelligence. Like a whettor whets the edges by rubbing objects on his wheel so should do the guru with

दर्पण के समान चमका दे ।।139।।

सतगुरू की महिमा अनँत, अनँत किया उपगार।
लोचन अनँत उघाड़िया, अनँत दिखावणहार।

गुरू की महिमा अपार है। उसके द्वारा किए गए उपकारों की कोई सीमा नहीं है। उसने मेरे अनन्त ज्ञान–चक्षु खोल दिए हैं और इस प्रकार मुझे वे परब्रह्म का साक्षात्कार कराने वाले हैं।।140।।

सतगुरू बपुरा क्या करै, जे सिषही मांहै चूक।
भावै त्यूं परबोध ले, ज्यूँ बंसि बजाई फूक।

अगर शिष्य में ही कमी है तो बेचारा सद्‌गुरू ही क्या कर सकता है ? उसे चाहे जिस प्रकार समझा दो,उस पर कोई स्थाई प्रभाव नहीं होता। जैसे वंशी में फूँक मारने से वह बजने लगती है, परंतु उसमें स्वर स्थायी नहीं होते, बजाने वाले अपने–अपने अनुकूल उसे बजा लेते हैं। वैसे ही व्यक्तित्व–शून्य शिष्य भी कभी एक के उपदेश पर चलता है, कभी दूसरे के।।141।।

सात समंद की मसि करौ, लेखनि सब बनराइ।
धरती सब कागद करौं, तऊं हरि गुण लिख्या न जाइ।

सातों समुद्रों को स्याही में तथा सम्पूर्ण वनों की लकड़ियों को कलम में परिणत कर लिया जाए और सम्पूर्ण धरती रूपी काग़ज़ पर भगवान् के गुणगान लिखें जाएँ, तब भी उनके पूरे गुण नहीं लिखे जा सकते हैं।।142।।

सुखिया सब संसार है, खायै अरू सौवै।
दुखिया दास कबीर है, जागै अरू रौवै।

सारा विषयी संसार सुखी है, खाता है और सोता है। केवल विरही कबीर दुःखी है जो जागता है और ईश्वर के विरह में रोता है।।143।।

the help of his enlightening words and incisive thoughts for his curious disciples to make their minds as clear as a shining mirror||139||

Satguru ki mahima ananta ananta kiya upakā r|
Lochan anant ughaariyā , ananta dikhavanhā r||

Infinite is Guru's glory; there is no end to his obligations on me. He has opened my inner eyes having infinite vision and now he is going to make me see the Ultimate||140||

Satguru bapura kyā kare, je sish hee mā he chook|
Bhā ve tyoon parabodhi le, jyon banshi bajai phook||

Poor real guru can't help either if his disciple has no capacity. In fact a disciple is like a flute sounding notes in accordance with the wind blown in, from the hole of his range||141||

Sat samand ki masi karon, lakhani sab banrai|
Dharati sab kagad karon, tahoon Hari run likyā na jai||

Even though ink be as much as the total capacity of the seven seas, pen be as many as the number of trees in all the jungles and the paper as much as much as the entire surface of the land of earth the glories of Lord(Hari) can't be written into totality||142||

Sukhia sab sansā r hai, khaye aur sove|
Dukhia dā s Kabir hai, jā ge aur rove||

The ignorant world eats drinks and sleeps merrily while Kabirda¯ s is an awakened soul that remains alert[but

सूरा तबही परषिये, लड़ै धणीं कै हेतु।
पुरिजा–पुरिजा ह्वै पड़ै, तऊ न छाड़ै खेत।

शूरवीर की परीक्षा उस समय होती है, जब वह अपने स्वामी के लिए लड़ता है। उस समय उसके अंग–अंग कट जाते हैं, परंतु वह फिर भी युद्ध–क्षेत्र नहीं छोड़ता है।।144।।

राम नाम जाण्यौं नहीं, लागी मोटी षोड़ि।
काया हाँड़ी काठ की, ना ऊँ चढ़े बहोड़ि।

अज्ञानी मानव, तूने इस जन्म में राम–नाम को जाना नहीं। तुझे बहुत बड़ा दूषण लग गया है, यह शरीर काठ की हँड़िया के समान है। उसे आग पर बार–बार नहीं चढ़ा सकते हैं।।145।।

राम नाम सब कोउ कहै, कहिबे बहुत बिचार।
सोइ रांम सत्ती कहै, सोई कौतिकहार।

राम–नाम का उच्चारण तो बहुत से करते हैं, पर कहने–करने में बहुत अन्तर है। अनन्य प्रेम वाली सती तथा सत्यनिष्ठ सन्त भी वही राम–नाम कहते हैं और बहरूपिया ढोंगी भी। ढोंगी कीर्तन के तमाशे का आनन्द लेता है, सन्त और सती की तरह नाम के मूल तत्त्व में मग्न नहीं होता। जो नाम का स्मरण इस मूल तत्व के साक्षात्कार सहित करता है, वही सती और सन्त है।।146।।

राम पियारा छांड़ि करि, करै आन का जाप।
बेस्यां केरा पूत ज्यूँ, कहैं कौन सूँ बाप।

जो परम प्रेमास्पद भगवान को छोड़कर अन्य देवताओं को जपता है, वह अनेक का भक्त होने के कारण वेश्या के पुत्र के समान है। वह किसी को भी अपना पिता नहीं कह सकता है।।147।।

लंबा मारग दूरि घर, विकट पंथ बहु मार।
कहौ संतो क्यूँ पाइये दुरलभ हरि दीदार।

realising the reality] and cries||143||

Soora tab hi parakhiye, larhe dhanee ke heta|
Purija-purija hve pade, tauoo na chhā de kheta||

A valiant is tested when to protect his master's interest he fights till the last drop of his blood and doesn't flee the battle field, even if his body be hacked to pieces||144||

Rām nām janyo nahin lagi motee shorhi|
Kāyā harhee kath ki, na uoon chade bahorhi||

O Man! If you fail to know about the virtues in the name of God you carry a big stigma. Remember that this body is like a wooden vessel which can't be used twice for cooking.[Hence don't waste this chance]||145||

Rām nām sab kauoo kahi, kahibe bahuta bichār|
Soi Ram satti kahe, soyee kantukhaar||

Though many chant Ram's name yet not with true feeling. Only men with total devtion-like the veridicious saints and sages do so. Otherwise those out of pure fun also chant this name. But the real realisation dawns in only those who do with total commitment||146||

Rām piyārā chadhi kari, kare āni kā jāp |
Vesyan kerā poota jyoon, kahe kaun soon baap||

Those who don't rely on beloved Rām and chant the names of other gods are like a son of a prostitute unable to identify his real father||147||

Lambā marag doori ghar, vikat panth bahu mār|
Kaho santo kyoon paiye durlabh Hari deedār||

ब्रह्मा तक पहुँचने का मार्ग बहुत लंबा है। (क्योंकि अनेक जन्मों के बाद मुक्ति प्राप्त होती है।) द्वैत–भावना, अज्ञान, विक्षेप, संशय आदि के अनेक व्यवधान बीच में आते हैं। अतः रास्ता भी अत्यन्त दुर्गम है। रास्ते में काम, क्रोध, लोभ आदि अनेक डाकू हैं। हे सन्तो, इस प्रकार के अत्यन्त दुर्लभ हरि–दर्शन को जीव सरलता से कैसे प्राप्त कर सकता है? ।।148।।

लूटि सकै तौ लूटियौ, राम नाम भंडार।
काल कंठ तै गहैया, रूधै दसूँ दुबार।

रामनाम के स्मरण का यह अक्षय भण्डार लूट सको तो लूट लो। (इस प्रकार इस पर अपना अधिकार कर लो।) फिर मृत्यु गले से दबोच ही लेगी और शरीर के दसों द्वार बंद हो जाएँगे। उस समय राम का स्मरण कौन करेगा ? और कैसे करेगा? ।।149।।

लूटि सकै तो लूटियौ, राम नाम है लूटि।
पीछे ही पछिताहुगे, यहु तन जैहि छूटि।

सब जगह रामनाम की लूट मची हुई है। अगर सामर्थ्य और सद्बुद्धि है तो ऐसे स्वर्ण–अवसर को छोड़ो मत, अन्यथा इस मानव शरीर के छूटने पर पश्चात्ताप करना पड़ेगा।।150।।

कुछ चुने हुए पद

1

का माँगू कछु थिर न रहाई,
देखन नैन चल्या जग जाइ!

एक लख पूत सवा लख नाती,
ता रावन घर दिया न दानी!
लंका–सो कोट समंद सी खाई,
ता रावन की खबर न पाई!

It is a long way, very dangerous and full of a variety of hazards. Saints! Tell me, is not God-realisation really so difficult and hence covered by a rare few?||148||

Looti sako tan lootiyo, Ram nam bhandār|
Kal kantha te gaharyyā, roondhe dason dwar||

Loot the treasure of God's name[chant as much as you like and own it]. Otherwise death will swipe at you like a vulture throttling all the perception-doors of the body. Then it will be too late to do so||149||

Loot sake tan lootiyo, Rām nām hai looti|
Peeche hee pachitā huge, yahu tan jaiyye chhooti||

All are looting the treasure of Ram's name. If you have capability and strength, don't let this golden opportunity be missed. Else, when you quit your mortal coil and your soul will repent loosing it||150||

Some Selected Verses

1.

Ka mangoon kachhu thir na rahāyee
Dekhata naina chalyā jag jāyee|

Ek lakh poota sava lakh nātee
Tā Rāvan ghar diya na batee
Lanka-so kot samanda-si khāyee
Ta Ravan ki khabar na payee

Aawat sanga na jat sangāti

आवन संग न जात संगानी,
कहा भयौ दरि बाँधें हाथी!
कहे कबीर अन्त की बारी,
हाथ झाँड़ि जैसे चले जुवारी!

अर्थः–

कबीर कहते हैं कि हे ईश्वर, मैं आपसे क्या माँगू, किस बात की इच्छा करूँ क्योंकि इस संसार में कुछ भी स्थायी नहीं है (हर चीज परिवर्तन शील है) जैसे [क्या रावण का वैभव स्थायी रह पाया?) जिस रावण के एक लाख पुत्र और सवा लाख नाती थे उसके घर में कोई दिया–बाती करने वाला (या परिवार का नाम चलाने वाला) भी नहीं रहा। उसका लका का दुर्ग विशाल था और समुद्र उसकी खाई जैसा था– लेकिन वह सब कुछ ऐसा नष्ट हुआ कि रावण का कोई नामोनिशान तक बाकी न रह पाया। इसलिए कबीर का कहना है कि इस संसार में न कोई साथ आता है। व्यक्तिगत वैभव जुटाना और दरवाजे पर हाथी बाँधने से क्या होता है जब कि अंत समय में तो सभी को अकेले ही जाना पड़ेगा। जिस प्रकार अपना सब कुछ आखिरी दाँव में लगा कर जुआरी बाजी हार कर अपने हाथ झाड़ता हुआ चला जाता है।

2.

झीनी–झीनी बीनी चदरिया!

काहे का ताना काहे की भरनी,
कौन तार से बीनी चदरिया?

इंगला पिंगला ताना भरनी,
सुखमन तार से बीनी चदरिया !

Kaha bhayo dar bandhe hāthee
Kahe Kabir ant ke bari
Hath jhārhi jaise chale juvari|

Meaning :

Says Kabir, O God, what should I desire from you since in this world nothing is permanent.[Everything is changeable]. For instance, the same Ravan who had a lakh of sons and a lakh and quarter grandsons eventually had no one to light a flame in the house[That is no one left to carry forward the family name]. His fort was very strong and the sea itself was like a moat to it. But all that was so totally destroyed that no trace was ultimately left of Ravan's family. In fact, every one comes in the world all alone and leaves it that way only. Hence there is hardly any sense in amassing wealth in this fey life or having elephants strutting at one's gate. Every one leaves like the gambler loosing everything in the end and rubbing empty hands in frustration.

2.

Jheeni-jheeni beeni chadariyā !

Kā he kā tā nā kahe ki bharani
Kaun tar se beeni chadariya?

Ingalā- pingalā tana bharani
Sushman tar se beeni chadariya!

Aath kanwal dus charkhā dole
Panchea tatva guna teeni chadariya
Nau-dus mas bunana men lage

आठ कँवल दस चरखा डोले,
पंच तत्त्व गुन तीनी चदरिया!
नौ दस–मास बुनन में लागे
ठोक–ठाक के बीनी चदरिया!

सो चादर सुर नर मुनि ओढ़ो
ओढ़ि कें मैली छीनी चदरिया।
दास कबीर जतन सों ओढ़ी
ज्यों की त्यों धरि दीनी चदरिया!

अर्थ:–

परमात्मा रूपी स्वामी ने मानव–रूपी चादर को बहुत बारीकि से बुना है। कबीर प्रश्न करते हैं कि यदि इस शरीर को चादर कहा जाता है तो फिर इसके ताने–बाने क्या हैं और किस तार से इसे बुना जाता है? उत्तर देते हुए वे कहते हैं कि 'इड़ा' तथा 'पिंगला' नाड़ियों के ताने बाने और सुषुम्ना के तार से यह शरीर रूपी चादर बुनी हुई है,

आठ चक्रों और दस रंध्रों रूपी चरखे पर कात कर इसे पाँच तत्त्वों और तीन गुणों से बनाया गया है। इसे बुनने में नौ–दस मास का समय लगता है ओर परमात्मा ने इसे काफी मजबूती से बुना है।

इस शरीर रूपी चादर को देवता, मनुष्य और मुनियों ने ओढ़ कर गन्दी या मैली कर दिया है परन्तु कबीर दास ने इसे जैसी की तैसी ओढ़ने के पश्चात् वापस कर दी है [अर्थात् उन्होंने इस को व्यर्थ नहीं किया है वरन् इसे अथत् ही वापस लौटा दिया है।]

3.

मन मस्त हुआ तब क्यों बोले

Thok-thāk ke beeni chadariyā!

So chadar sur-nar-muni odhee
Odhi ken mailee keeni chadariyā!
Dās Kabir jatan sen odhee
Jyon ki tyon dhari deeni chadariyā!

Meaning :
God has knitted the sheet of cloth of the human form with great and subtle distinction. Kabir questions that if this human form is likened to sheet of cloth how it has been warped and wefted and with what thread? Answering himself he says that with the warp and weft of Idā and Pinglā nerves the cloth-sheet like human body has been spun by God on the thread of Sushamna [1]. Mounted on the wheel having eight circles[2] and ten holes[3] this sheet has been spun with the help of five elements [4] and three [5] basic categories of the quality. About 9 to 10 months are need to make ready and such sheet(human body) since God spins it in quite a gruff and strong way. This sheet has been used as a cover by men, gods and sages but they have defiled it. It is only Kabirdās who has used it and returned it as it was given to him[i.e., He has not wasted human life and quitted his mortal coil with any blemish on it]

3.

Man masta huaā tab kyon bole?

1. Ida, Pingla and Sushmna are the basic nerves of the human body that awaken the dorment super natural powers in human by the belief of the Hath yoga.
2. The eight donment sources of particular adaptness that bhoom when the Kundalini is awekened.
3. Ten openings in the body.

हीरा पायो गाँठ गठायो
बार–बार बाकों क्या खोले?

हलकी थी तब चढ़ी तराजू
पूरी भई तब क्यों तोले?

हंसा पाए मान सरोवर
ताल तलैया क्यों डोले?

तेरा साहब है घर माही
बाहर नैना क्यों खोले
कहें कबीर सुनो भाई साधो
साहब मिल गए तिल ओले।

अर्थः–

कबीर दास कहते हैं कि जब मन परमानन्द में मग्न हो गया है तो अब वह (बाहरी दुनियाँ से) बोल के क्या पाएगा?

अब उसे आत्मज्ञान या ब्रहमज्ञान रूपी हीरा मिल गया है तो बार–बार उसे वह खोल कर क्यों दिखाए?

जब हँस को मानसरोवर मिल ही गया है तो छोटे–छोटे तालों और तालाबों में उसके डोलने से क्या प्रयोजन? अर्थात् उसे अब ऐसा करने की कोई आवश्यकता नहीं।

कबीर कहते हैं कि शरीर रूपी दुर्ग का स्वामी अर्थात् ईश्वर मनुष्य के भीतर ही बिराजमान है इसलिए उसे बाहर भटकने की कोई जरूरत नहीं। उसे बाहर क्या खोजना जो स्वयं मन के भीतर ही विद्यमान है?

Heerā payo gantha gathāyo
Bar-Bar bakon kyon khole?

Halki thee tab chadhee tarāju
Poori bhayee tab kyā tole?
Hansa payo Mansarovar
Tāl-tallaiyyā kyon dole?

Tera saheb hai ghar mānhi
Bahar naina kyon khole?
Kahen Kabir suno bhai sadho
Saheb mil gaye til ole!

Meaning :

Kabir das says that when mind receives the supreme bless why must it become extrovent and indulge in the wordly affairs.

When it has received the supreme gem of God-realisation why must it show repeated by to the world outside?

When the swan has attained to the divine lake of Mansarovar, its very origin, where is the sense in its searching for ordinary ponds and puddles?

Says Kabir that the owner of the soul resides in the body itself and hence there is hardly any need for the mind to wander for it outside. Why must it go on searching something which is available inside home?

4. Five basic element.

5. Three basic categories: Sattvik, Rajas, Tamasik.